MORE MEMORIES OF
EDINBURGH

The publishers would like to thank the following companies for their

support in the production of this book

Main Sponsor

VA TECH Elin Transformers, Edinburgh

Aitken & Niven

Isis Asset Management

The Link Group

Edinburgh's Telford College

Thomas Marin Funeral Directors

First published in Great Britain by True North Books Limited
England HX3 6AE
01422 344344

ISBN 1 903204 72 0

Text, design and origination by True North Books Limited
Printed and bound by The Amadeus Press Limited

MORE MEMORIES OF
EDINBURGH

By courtesy of Edinburgh City Libraries

Contents

Introduction

With its unforgettable castle and its setting amongst dramatic crags Edinburgh, capital of Scotland, appears timeless. Yet it has experienced all the slings and arrows of capricious fortune, and the city has continually renewed itself: today it is a major centre for government and finance, tourism, and cultural affairs. The origin of Edinburgh is shrouded in myth. The lack of authentic information has however been made up for by tradition, etymology, and conjecture. It is widely believed that the city derives its name from Edwin a 7th century Northumbrian king; it was called Edwinesburch by Simon of Durham, who mentions it as existing in the eighth century; and in the charter of foundation of the Abbey of Holyrood in 1128 it is mentioned as the king's burg of Edwinesburg. In Gaelic the name is Dun-Edin, or 'fort on the hill slope', a designation given in the Register of the Priory of St. Andrews, dated 1107. The city owes its origin to its castle, called in numerous Latin charters Castrum Puellarum, the Maidens' Castle - fabled to have been the residence of young Pictish princesses. Descriptions of Edinburgh at various periods offer a fascinating contrast to the present city. In 1255 Margaret, Queen of Alexander III, complained to the Scottish estates, that she was confined in the Castle 'a sad and solitary place without verdure and by reason of its vicinity to the sea unwholesome.' In 1384-5 the houses of the town were described as having thatched roofs, and at that time did not exceed four hundred. The city however continued to grow: in 1478 the Duke of Gloucester, afterwards Richard III, camped nearby, and described it as a place of opulence. By the beginning of the sixteenth century Edinburgh could boast of many churches and monasteries; in 1615 Taylor, the Water Poet, called the High Street the 'fairest and goodliest street his eyes ever beheld, the buildings on each side being all of squared stone, five, six, and seven storeys high and many by-lanes and closes on each side of the way wherein are gentlemen's houses much fairer than the High Street'. The

history of Edinburgh however is intimately entwined with that of Scotland itself. In the reign of David II, 1329-71, Edinburgh was considered one of the chief towns of the kingdom.

The town contributed 50,000 marks for the ransom of James I in 1424 who in gratitude made it his residence. It became the capital after James' assassination in 1437, being considered more secure than any other town. James III was crowned in the city and here his marriage with Mary of Gueldres was celebrated with great magnificence in 1449.

In 1469 James III was married at Edinburgh to Margaret of Denmark: it was he who presented the city with a banner popularly known as the Blue Blanket, long-preserved in the Trades Maidens Hospital. James IV enlivened the city by the splendid tournaments he held. In 1532 James V instituted the supreme legal tribunal of Scotland, the College of Justice or Court of Session in Edinburgh, in imitation, it is said, of the Parliament of Paris. In 1516 Queen Mary entered Edinburgh on her arrival from France it became a backdrop to her tragic life. James VI, Mary's son, was born in Edinburgh Castle in 1566; he left Edinburgh to go southward on his accession to the crown of England in 1603. James' son Charles I visited Edinburgh in 1633 and again in 1641. It was during his reign within St Giles Church that the noted Jenny Geddes threw her cutty stool at the head of the Dean of Edinburgh who was reading the Liturgy then being forced upon the Scottish people. Oliver Cromwell took possession of the city in 1650. In 1745 Prince Charles Edward Stuart flew his banner above quarters in the Palace of Holyrood. The Georgian-style New Town arose in the late 18th and 19th centuries, made possible in part by the draining of the Nor' Loch, which stood at the base of Castle Rock. The city expanded also to the south of the Old Town, beyond the Meadows, which occupy the site of the drained South Loch. Today, in the 21st century, at the beginning of the third millennium, this book is dedicated to all those readers who take unashamed pleasure in nostalgia. This is not however the kind of dry, boring history book which so many of us were made to study in our long-gone school days: instead it is a vivid reminder of our own history. Here within this book's covers can be found images of 20th century Edinburgh, from times now just on the edge of living memory, to what may seem like the day before yesterday - until we gasp with astonishment that 20 years or more have inexplicably elapsed since we last looked on

By courtesy of Edinburgh City Libraries

a scene depicted here. This carefully chosen collection of photographs, with their memory-jogging text, will bring smiles of happiness, and perhaps some tears too, with their evocations of life in Edinburgh in the middle decades of what is now 'the last century'. Are you old enough to remember the war years? Can you recall sitting at home in 1939 listening to Mr Chamberlain's announcement that Herr Hitler had declined to withdraw from Poland and that as a consequence we were at war with Germany for a second time, after just 21 years of peace? Or are you a little younger: do you perhaps recall the young Queen Elizabeth's coronation in 1953 and the excitement of street parties to celebrate the event? Maybe you are old enough to have experienced the electrifying thrill of hearing rock and roll music for the first time in the mid 1950s and joining in the worldwide acclaim for that astonishingly gifted young man Elvis Presley. Readers who are younger still will find their memories jogged with pictures of the swinging sixties. Who amongst those who lived through those years can ever forget the Beatles, the Rolling Stones, mini skirts, the arrival of Radio One, colour television and, gloriously capping the decade, that historic landing on the Moon by American astronauts? Is it really now more than 30 years ago that Neil Armstrong said those famous words 'That's one small step for man, one giant leap for mankind'? Was it really as far back as 1979 that Margaret Thatcher became Prime Minister? Goodness how the years fly by.

But though world-changing events and internationally famous faces may be important it is the everyday lives of ordinary folk which ultimately matter most. It is personal memories of life in Edinburgh which will inevitably be jogged most vigorously by the contents of this book: our schooldays, our first job; the happiness of a first stolen kiss on the back row of the cinema, juxtaposed with the inevitable sadness of recollecting names and faces long gone. So go and make yourself a nice cup of tea and plump up the cushions of your favourite armchair. Gather your friends and family around you and delve deep into not only the history of Edinburgh but your own history too. There's nothing wrong with nostalgia, especially today when even folk well on their way to middle age can no longer recall that 75p once meant fifteen shillings! Yes, history can mean events of a thousand years ago, but in truth history began yesterday. So sit back and enjoy this unique book about our Edinburgh, an Edinburgh which still continues to exist in our memories and be cherished in all our hearts.

MAULES

Street Scenes

Photographed in Edwardian days the West End of Princes Street looking east presents a curious sight to modern eyes. In some respects the view is clearly the same, not least the skyline which remains substantially unaltered thanks to enlightened planners and the lesser attentions of Herr Hitler and the Luftwaffe, who between them all but destroyed so much of Britain's other historic city centres. Happily for posterity this view remains readily recognisable though the differences are as startling as the similarities. The fleet of flat-topped trams ambling along like a herd of pachyderms, though a new addition to the scene when this photo was taken, have been gone for five decades, and when did you last see a dog cart being driven along the road? What is most wonderful to see is the pedestrians who act as if they, not the motorcar, own the road. That slow pace of life meant that all but the most elderly and infirm always had ample time to cross the street; the lightning reflexes required of today's motorists were not a prerequisite for driving a horse along the road. The white-gloved traffic policeman in the centre of the picture looks as if he might be at risk of being run down by the tram headed straight for him, but since the trams travelled little faster than walking pace, in truth he has more than enough time to step out of the way. Today anyone who steps out into Princes Street needs to be very nimble on their feet indeed.

This very old photograph, taken in 1901, shows North Bridge with the North British Hotel still under construction. The hotel was opened the following year by the North British Railway Company. The hotel's 55-metre tall clock tower with its clock always kept two minutes fast would become an Edinburgh landmark. The building was sold in 1981 and was reopened as the Balmoral Hotel in 1991. To the right of the hotel, with its distinctive dome, is the classical façade of the Register House which houses the Scottish Record Office. Built between 1774 and 1827 mainly from designs drawn up by the Edinburgh-educated Robert Adam, its principle function is to 'preserve and provide access to our national archival heritage'. The result - written records dating back to the twelfth century concerning the kingdom of Scotland are lodged here. The Register House also is the repository of Government, church and legal records as well as estate and family documents. On a lighter note James Tyler a local journalist made the first manned hot air balloon ascent on the British mainland from the Comely Garden: prior to that ascent he had practiced with his great fire balloon actually within the shell of the Register House which was then under construction. Meanwhile, along the road, everything speaks of a tranquillity unknown in this modern age, nothing faster than a tram is in sight, there are more pedestrians than wheeled vehicles and one cyclist on his way towards the camera has even dismounted as if even pedal power is too fast for him.

Events of the 1930s

MELODY MAKERS
Throughout the 1930s a young American trombonist called Glenn Miller was making his mark in the world of music. By 1939 the Glenn Miller sound was a clear leader in the field; his clean-cut, meticulously executed arrangements of numbers such as 'A String of Pearls' and 'Moonlight Serenade' brought him fame across the world as a big-band leader. During a flight to England from Paris in 1944 Miller's plane disappeared; no wreckage was ever found.

INVENTION AND TECHNOLOGY
With no driving tests or speed restrictions, 120,000 people were killed on the roads in Britain between the two world wars. In 1934 a Halifax man, Percy Shaw, invented a safety device destined to become familiar the world over: reflecting roadstuds. In dark or foggy conditions the studs that reflected light from the car's headlights kept traffic on the 'straight and narrow' and must over the years have saved many lives.

SCIENCE AND DISCOVERY
By observing the heavens, astronomers had long believed that there in the constellation of Gemini lay a new planet, so far undiscovered. They began to search for the elusive planet, and a special astronomical camera was built for the purpose. The planet Pluto was discovered by amateur astronomer Clyde Tombaugh in 1930, less than a year later.

By courtesy of Edinburgh City Libraries

Here's as fine a sight as it's possible to see: the west end of Princes Street in a photograph dated 1937. What a wealth of detail there is here to delight the eye. In many ways the view has barely changed at all in the intervening decades: on the right can be seen the north side of the 19th century church of St John, whilst in the distance can be seen the 190 ft high Scott Monument erected in 1844 in memory of Sir Walter Scott at a cost if £15,650. In the far distance one can just make out the never to be finished Greek style national monument to the dead of the Napoleonic wars begun in 1822. Princes Street was completed in 1805 as part of the New Town scheme and was named after Prince George, later to become George IV. The street's distinction lies not so much in its width, nor in its mile-long straightness, but in the trees and gardens and distinguished buildings which flank its southern side. This busy photograph appears to have been taken from the first floor of the Caledonian Hotel and shows how even so many decades ago Princes Street was just as busy as it is today. But there are of course many noticeable differences from today's scene: the trams are sadly long gone whilst the cars and lorries which fill the road are all what we now consider to be vintage vehicles. Another vintage feature is the traffic directing policemen with his white armbands to make him more visible to motorists. With ever increasing numbers of traffic lights being installed the traffic policeman would became a rare sight indeed by the 1970s.

By courtesy of Edinburgh City Libraries

What a wonderful scene captured in the early months of 1953. The location is Princes Street at its junction with the Mound. To the left is the corner of the Royal Scottish Academy, overhead, criss-crossing the road like filaments of a giant spider's web, are the wires providing electricity to the city's trams. Eerily masked by mist, looms Edinburgh Castle, hardly discernable yet still unmistakable. What are the folk walking over Edinburgh's cobbled streets on this misty morn talking about? There was certainly plenty to talk about in that year, now over half a century ago: In January Eisenhower had become 34th President of the USA - just in time to bid farewell to Joseph Stalin who died in March at the age of 74.

Though Marshall Stalin, under the benevolent guise of 'Uncle Joe', had been Britain and America's wartime ally in the struggle against Hitler during the second world war, it had always been an uneasy relationship: many regarded Stalin as an even worse and more dangerous dictator than the late and unlamented Fuhrer had been. With Stalin's death many in the West heaved a sigh of relief, though it would not be for many more decades that the Cold War would begin to thaw and the collapse of the Soviet Union showed Communism to have been a brave but failed experiment. Meanwhile back in 1953 Edinburgh one vestige of the second world war had at last ended: on 4th February, to the delight of every youngster and dentist, sweet rationing finally ceased.

Below: Despite its appearance this is not just any old mobile café; in fact this is an official Ministry of Food 'transportable kitchen unit' at the Civil Defence Emergency Feeding Demonstration held at Springfield House, Edinburgh in October 1953. Everyone is enjoying a bowl of hot soup: well almost everyone, the couple on the left of the scene look less than pleased, perhaps the only flavour on offer is one they don't like. Or perhaps they, like many others, are contemplating what 'Civil Defence' is really all about. Youngsters imagined that when the second war ended in 1945 the world would be at peace. Older folk knew better. No sooner had the second world war finished than the Cold War broke out. The Allies had finished off Herr Hitler and the Japanese but now fear arose that our wartime ally Russia would continue to roll eastwards and engulf the west. We had hoped that our atom bombs might save us from the Communists, but it was a short-lived dream, soon turned into a nightmare. Joseph Stalin the Russian leader might have died in March 1953 but his legacy continued, and by August 1953 the USSR had exploded its own hydrogen bomb. Years of fear would follow, and with that fear came the need to maintain a Civil Defence capability to meet the country's needs in the event of renewed war. Many however felt that if nuclear bombs began to drop there would be few left to appreciate a reviving cup of tea afterwards.

Right: It was a dull day in 1953 when the cameraman looked down on Edinburgh's Long Stairs and snapped these folk catching their breaths and counting the steps. The picture wonderfully captures so many elements of Edinburgh denied to citizens of lesser cities: solid stone, hills and dramatic vistas. Changing times however are represented here by the gas lamp at the bottom of the stairs; ornate gas lamps were systematically replaced during the 1960s, all too often with unattractive but cheap concrete pillars. Yet the old gas lamps are fondly remembered by those who climbed them, played cricket against them and did their courting beneath them. Sadly this gas lamp has its glass missing, no doubt knocked out by vandals and never to be replaced: the future, electric lighting can be seen on the left where a spotlight can be made out on the wall. But what of that strange feature over the doorway on the right? Is it another light of some kind or perhaps a siren to warn of air raids - reminders of the war. So many things were different half a century ago. Look at the lady in the centre of the scene; she's wearing a fur coat and no doubt very happy to be doing so. By the late 20th century animal rights activists had made fur coats deeply unfashionable amongst those who cared about animal suffering: in 1953 having a fur coat was still something to aim for, it not only kept its wearer superbly warm but also declared that its owner was someone to be reckoned with.

In 1955 the cameraman stood in the centre of Cowgate and pointed his camera towards the setting sun capturing forever this wonderfully evocative picture of historic Grassmarket and Edinburgh Castle beyond. A focal point of Old Town, the Grassmarket had been an actual cattle market for five hundred years until the start of the 20th century. And what a tale its cobble stones could tell if only they could speak: this was a place of execution with more than 100 Covenanters who died here, commemorated by a monument at the eastern end of the market where once the gallows stood. It was just off the western end of Grassmarket in no-longer existing Tanner's Close that Irishmen Burke and Hare, the notorious murderers who killed their victims in order to sell the bodies to surgeons, once lived. The wicked pair killed some 16 victims before being caught: Hare turned King's evidence and was subsequently set free, Burke was hanged on 28th January 1829 and himself dissected by the medical profession. Burke was not as lucky as Maggie Dickson who a century earlier had been hanged for concealing the death of her child. During a dispute over her body between friends who wanted to give her a decent burial and medical students who wanted to dissect her Maggie suddenly came back to life - and having already been declared dead was spared the ordeal of a second hanging. Maggie lived for another 30 years and the Grassmarket pub Maggie Dickson's commemorates the curious tale of 'Half-hangit Maggie' to this day.

Events of the 1950s

WHAT'S ON?
Television hit Britain in a big way during the 1950s. Older readers will surely remember 'Double Your Money, Dixon of Dock Green and 'Dragnet' (whose characters' names were changed 'to protect the innocent'). Commercial television was introduced on 22nd September 1955, and Gibbs SR toothpaste was drawn out of the hat to become the first advert to be shown. Many believed adverts to be vulgar, however, and audiences were far less than had been hoped for.

GETTING AROUND
The year 1959 saw the development of the world's first practical air-cushion vehicle - better known to us as the hovercraft. The earliest model was only able to travel at slow speeds over very calm water and was unable to carry more than three passengers. The faster and smoother alternative to the sea ferry quickly caught on, and by the 1970s a 170-ton car-carrying hover-craft service had been introduced across the English Channel.

SPORTING CHANCE
The four-minute mile had remained the record since 1945, and had become regarded as virtually unbreakable. On 6th May 1954, however, Oxford University student Roger Bannister literally ran away with the record, accomplishing the seemingly impossible in three min-utes 59.4 seconds. Bannister col-lapsed at the end of his last amaz-ing lap, even temporarily losing his vision. By the end of the day, how-ever, he had recovered sufficiently to celebrate his achievement in a London night club!

Victorian Britain's vision of itself as the new Roman Empire is vividly illustrated here with the sight, in the distance, of the National Monument, the largest structure on the summit of Calton Hill to the east of the city. This over ambitious attempt to equal or indeed better the Parthenon of Athens was intended to honour Scotsmen who fell fighting Napoleon in the early years of the 19th century. Money was raised by public subscription and its construction began in 1822 some seven years after Napoleon's final defeat at Waterloo and his exile to St Helena. Money ran out after just 12 columns were competed and the monument became known as 'Edinburgh's Disgrace'. Today the very fact that the monument remains uncompleted lends it such curiosity value that few now would ever propose to compete the project. This photograph looking east along Princes Street was taken in 1956, almost as the death knell of the old tramway system was being rung. Because of extensive road works all the traffic has been directed on to the northern side of the road leaving the southern sets visible all the way to the Scott Monument. The patchwork of earlier repairs in tar macadam testifies to a certain amount of parsimony on behalf of the civic authorities during this period. Alas, today few will ever see Princes Street so quiet: today's dual carriageway with its pelican crossings and endless traffic makes the road seem more like a madhouse than the apparently tranquil thoroughfare pictured here.

It's a fine sunny morning here at Canonmills on the north side of the city. The year is 1958 and outside McGlashen Fireplace Specialists a small queue has formed to await the next bus. What might those folk waiting at the bus stop be discussing on this glorious day? Perhaps they are sharing a view popular with many that all those space rockets are doing funny things to the weather. Though in the 21st century global warming is the prime suspect for any type of unseasonable weather, back in the 1950s, the Americans and Russians were getting all the credit and the blame: the USSR's Sputnik I had been sent into orbit back in early January but by the end of the month the Americans had matched them with their Explorer satellite: the race for space was on! The concrete lampposts in the centre of the scene hint at modernity but almost everything else tells of days now long past. Today the two ornate iron lampposts are museum pieces, or would be used as a the pattern for modern retro style street furniture so beloved of those who want to recreated that 'heritage' feel - but these objects are the real thing. Most startling of all to modern eyes is the road itself: not only is it covered in stone sets but upon them are laid tram tracks along which a tram will never appear. Perhaps however the most remarkable aspect of the scene is the utter absence of a motorcar - an absence made even more remarkable by the fact that the Canonmills Garage is so prominently pictured.

Above: Tiny road signs like the one on the left directing motorists to the A1, or the Great North Road as it was still known in the 1950s, would not be much use to today's motorists. In the 21st century busy roads and faster speeds mean car drivers need far larger direction signs if they are to avoid getting lost. In 1958 however when this scene at Canonmills was captured by the photographer speed was hardly a problem. Indeed trying to get up speed on cobbles was not particularly advisable since the vibrations coming up through the floor would be enough to loosen the teeth in a driver's head, not to mention parts being shaken free from the unfortunate vehicle. The driver of the car parked on the right of this scene had many fewer problems than today's harassed motorists - no double yellow lines for a start; those few fortunate enough to own a car of their own could usually park exactly where they wanted - right outside the shop of their choice - oh happy days! Some things however seem never to have changed - not least the Coca Cola sign outside the shop on the left. America's Coca Cola drink is usually thought of as a very modern import to Scotland yet bottles (and back then they were proper thick glass bottles, none of your plastic) of 'Coke' had been on sale for many years. Coca-Cola was invented by Atlanta pharmacist John Pemberton in response to the US state of Georgia introducing prohibition in 1885; by 1905 it was being marketed as 'the Great temperance Drink'.

Here's a fine view of the Mound captured in 1959. In the distance can be seen Princes Street, to the left are West Princes Street Gardens and to the right the site of the National Gallery. Several years have passed since the last tram made its way across the Mound but as is the way with things no-one has yet got around to removing the tram tracks which are still fixed in the roadbed. Buses have now completely replaced Edinburgh's trams two of which can be seen here making their way across the massive embankment which has linked the New Town to the Old Town since the 19th century, cutting in half what was once the Nor' Loch. Though rounding the bend are a number of cars which have already given sterling service to their owners the foreground tells us that modern times are approaching: Henry Ford famously said of his Model T that it was available in any colour so long as it was black; now however cars are becoming available in a greater range of colour and more exciting styles. Is that a Hillman Hunter just turning off into Market Street? And right in the centre of the picture is that famous British stalwart the Morris Minor apparently with its driver's foot to floor attempting to overtake the two cars in front by hurtling up the tram tracks. The Morris Minor was one of the true greats of British motoring and Britain's highly successful answer to the Volkswagen Beetle.

By courtesy of Edinburgh City Libraries

Above: The beautiful Princes Street Gardens, the green lungs at the heart of the city of Edinburgh, lie in the narrow valley which was once the boggy depression known as the Nor' Loch. That wet wasteland was drained in the early 19th century as part of the development which led to the New Town which grew to the north of Edinburgh Castle. The Princes Street Gardens are split in the middle by The Mound where some two million cart-loads of earth and rock were dumped during the construction of the New Town, in the process providing a new link road across what had been the Nor' Loch to the Old Town. Completed in 1830 The Mound was soon a major thoroughfare though it would not remain undisturbed forever. As in every other street in Edinburgh The Mound too would eventually be improved for the benefit of motor transport. In 1959 it was decided to lower the road level, an event captured for posterity in this photograph of the road works which followed that decision. Perhaps the most startling feature of this photograph is the compete absence of mechanisation. Today any similar building site would inevitably feature a large mechanical digger as its central focus, but here in 1959 shovels and wheelbarrows are still very much the order of the day. Only the snaking hose of a pneumatic drill on the right of the picture gives any hint that working practices have changed significantly since droves of navvies carrying shovels and picks arrived in Edinburgh to build the railway a century earlier

Events of the 1950s

HOT OFF THE PRESS

The 1950s seemed to be the heyday of spies, and in 1951 the activities of Guy Burgess and Donald Maclean caused a sensation in the country. Both had occupied prominent positions in the Foreign Office, while Burgess had also been a member of MI-6. Recruited by the Russians while at Cambridge University in the 1930s, the traitors provided the Soviets with a huge amount of valuable information. They disappeared in 1951, surfacing in Moscow five years later.

THE WORLD AT LARGE

Plans to develop the economies of member states into one common market came to fruition on 1st January 1958, when the EEC came into operation. The original members were France, Belgium, Luxembourg, The Netherlands, Italy, and West Germany. The Community became highly successful, achieving increased trade and prosperity across Western Europe while at the same time alleviating fear of war which lingered on after the end of World War II. Britain became a member in 1973.

ROYAL WATCH

King George VI's health had been causing problems since 1948, when he developed thrombosis. In 1951 the King - always a heavy smoker - became ill again, and was eventually found to be suffering from lung cancer. His left lung was removed in September of 1951. In January 1952 he waved Princess Elizabeth and Prince Philip off on their tour of Africa; they were never to see him again. The King died on 5th February 1952.

By courtesy of Edinburgh City Libraries

It's a quarter to nine in the evening looking west along Princes Street from Waterloo Place. The cameraman has succeeded in capturing an unusual conjunction of lights, not only from the sunset but also from the street lights and the glare reflected on the soon-to-be-gone tram lines. This almost magical moment was captured on film in 1955. Perhaps the cameraman had another kind of light in mind when he took this photo. The atomic bomb was ten years old and its awesome power was still on everyone's mind. In fact plans to harness nuclear power for peaceful means were what the government wanted minds to be focussed on, plans for no fewer than 12 nuclear power stations to provide 'clean and almost unlimited electricity' had just been unveiled. But so had plans to proceed to build hydrogen bombs even more powerful that the atom bombs which had destroyed Hiroshima and Nagasaki on the 6th and 9th of August 1945 bringing the war against Japan to a sudden halt with Japan's unconditional surrender on 14th of August. But whilst the likelihood of mushroom clouds of the atomic kind appeared to be increasing other kinds of cloud were on the verge of disappearing: in London the first smokeless zones were introduced, something which would be phased in over the whole of Britain in the next decade. One curious consequence would be less spectacular sunsets as less smoke and dust filled the atmosphere - though what sunsets there were would become more easily seen!

It's 1956 and a coach has parked at the side of the
Old Waverley Hotel to discharge its passengers.
On the left is a corner of the Scott Monument
built to commemorate Sir Walter Scott after his
death in 1832. In addition to the statue of Scott
himself, carved from a 30-ton block of Italian marble,
the stone figures in niches around the monument's base
represent characters from Scott's novels. Scott's
favourite dog Bevis attends his master under the great
stone canopy. Completed in 1844 the designer of the
extraordinarily ornate monument was GM Kemp, a self-
taught architect who sadly did not live to see the
project finished. The year 1956 was a turning point in
the Edinburgh street scene, since that was the year that

its trams ran for the last time. Though the tram tracks would remain in situ sometimes for many years, in other parts of the city, they would disappear here rather more quickly. In the distance in this photograph can be seen two corporation buses, highly functional, but never to be as well loved as the old trams they replaced. The stone sets which feature so prominently in this scene are soon to be history too. Already patched with tar macadam that blacktop road covering would soon spread like bacteria in a laboratory Petrie dish to eventually obliterate the old stone beneath. Car drivers inevitably approved of the smother ride, but even they recognised that something of Edinburgh's character disappeared beneath the tar and chippings.

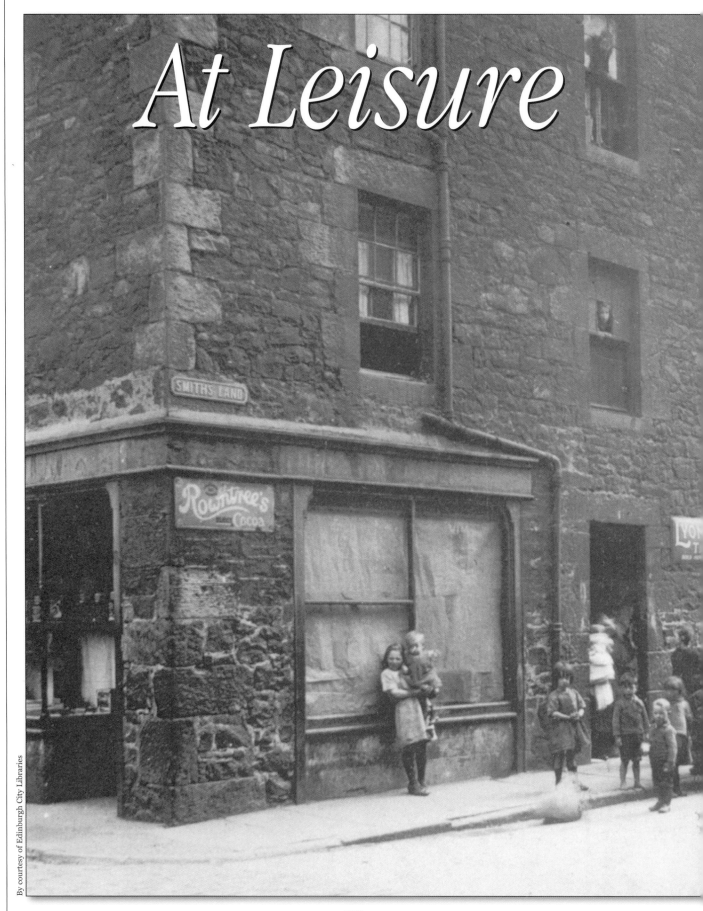

At Leisure

How many readers recognise this scene we wonder? Not many we expect, though as a general illustration of the times in the hungry thirties it will be a familiar one to older readers who lived through those grim days. The street is Smiths Land off Harthorn Bank, South Queensferry. Thousands of folk were born, lived and died in similar terraces of four storied houses, with corner shops at the end of the road. Today, enamelled adverts, such as those seen here promoting Rowntrees Cocoa and Lyons Tea are much sought after collectors' items, so much so that new ones are still being made. Thousands of similar homes were build in the late 19th century - and just look at those corner stones, don't they just look as if they've been built to last? This, alas, is a scene which can never be repeated: the volume of road traffic means that playing in the street is a thing of the past, never again will women hang their washing out in the street on Mondays, never again will youngsters build bonfires on the cobbles to celebrate November 5th , and no more can excited boys enjoy the excitement of striking clog irons on sets to emit a shower of sparks from their feet. Nor can mothers and fathers sit on the doorsteps on warm summers evenings drinking tea, keeping an eye on the youngsters and sharing gossip with neighbours: the push of traffic and the pull of television makes us all less sociable these days.

Below: In 1948 standing in the open air was the no-choice option for the majority of this crowd of rugby fans; these days Murrayfield offers an all-covered venue with seats for crowds of up to 67,000; but though the facilities may have been improved the atmosphere of the old stands will never be bettered. The modern 'Braveheart' blue warpaint and flags draped around bodies are conspic-uous by their absence from this crowd whilst the lone police sergeant can enjoy the game without to many worries about the self-disciplined crowd which in those days largely policed itself. Following all the long partings, hardships and deprivations of the second world war attendances at sporting events were huge: folk were determined to make up for all the lost years. And that determina-tion is reflected in the huge crowd to be seen at this Murrayfield international against the 'auld enemy'. Anticipation is high as the ball runs loose near the English try line. Exactly one hundred years before this match was captured by the cameraman, Scotland's first senior rugby match was

played between Edinburgh Academicals and a university team. In 1848 the rules were however somewhat different: that game had involved 50 players and lasted four days! Murrayfield was opened in 1924 replacing Inverleith as the venue for internationals. Though the game has not changed much since this scene much else has: the sight of invalids and injured war veterans seated close to the touchline with rugs over their knees is now just a memory.

Left: Three smart lads pose for the camera in this picture from the late 1950s, bringing memories of our school days flooding back. The first thing to strike us is just how smart the little lads were, despite the fact that money was tight and it was not always easy to find cash to spend on clothing. Still, people did the best with what they had, homemade haircuts and hand-me-down clothes made up for the lack of money when the need arose. The picture highlights just how much fashions have changed since the era featured here. Try getting your little lad to wear short trousers and white ankle socks... let alone a tie!

The 1950s and the wonder and excitement of the acquisition of the first television set. Black and white of course and though this model was not one of the cheapest sets available then, the screen was probably only a modest twelve or fourteen inches. People then considered television a mere adjunct to radio and even the design of this set makes it look like a wireless. It may well have been acquired to enable the family (and others) to watch the Queen's Coronation in 1953. The dress of the young ladies admiring the set epitomises the 1950s, as does the small table lamp standing on its own 'mat' - so as not to damage this expensive and prized new piece of furniture.

Events of the 1940s

WHAT'S ON?

In wartime Britain few families were without a wireless set. It was the most popular form of entertainment, and programmes such as ITMA, Music While You Work and Workers' Playtime provided the people with an escape from the harsh realities of bombing raids and ration books. In 1946 the BBC introduced the Light Programme, the Home Service and the Third Programme, which gave audiences a wider choice of listening.

GETTING AROUND

October 1948 saw the production of Britain's first new car designs since before the war. The Morris Minor was destined for fame as one of the most popular family cars, while the four-wheel-drive Land Rover answered the need for a British-made off-road vehicle. The country was deeply in the red, however, because of overseas debts incurred during the war. The post-war export drive that followed meant that British drivers had a long wait for their own new car.

SPORTING CHANCE

American World Heavyweight Boxing Champion Joe Louis, who first took the title back in 1937, ruled the world of boxing during the 1930s and 40s, making a name for himself as unbeatable. Time after time he successfully defended his title against all comers, finally retiring in 1948 after fighting an amazing 25 title bouts throughout his boxing career. Louis died in 1981 at the age of 67.

Wartime

Below: A proud father poses for the camera with his latest arrival. The baby had not arrived from Mars, in fact the 'arrival' was not a baby at all, but an anti-gas attack suit which was compulsory for babies in the United Kingdom during the Second World War. An air pump at the side of the suit enabled anxious parents to replenish the supply of air to the precious package inside. It is said that most babies were less than enthusiastic abut the prospect of being encased in the suit - and who could blame them? The picture was taken in 1939. In the event there was never any gas attack on British soil during the course of the Second World War.

Bottom: The Women's Voluntary Service was founded as a Civil Defence auxiliary unit in 1938. The WVS gained much experience in providing emergency meals during the second world war, often using the most primitive equipment. WVS mobile canteens served the forces both at home and abroad. During the war years the WVS gained an unforgettable reputation amongst both members of the armed forces and those whose homes had been bombed, always ensuring that cups of tea, sandwiches and cakes were provided exactly where they were needed. When the war ended however members of the WVS had acquired a taste for public service and were unwilling simply to close shop. Distributing Meals on Wheels on a regular basis to needy people, particularly the elderly, after the war was a new challenge, but one the organisation readily adapted to. In the first six months of 1958, the year when this photograph was taken, the WVS delivered 75,000 such meals - the first course always piping hot from 'Hot Lock' containers. The Edinburgh Central members of the WVS are looking delighted at the acquisition of two brand new

vans. The fully-fitted vehicles named Cowan and Hanover are gaining the seal of approval from two key figures in WVS: standing in front of the bonnet of Hanover are, from right to left, Mrs Marshal the Meals on Wheels organiser for Edinburgh Central, and Lady MacColl, Chairman of WVS Scotland. Things had moved a long way from the immediate post-war years when members often delivered meals in their own vehicles.

Left: War had been declared, and every citizen of Britain, young and old, male and female, was called upon to put his or her back into the war effort. Those who did not go into military service of one kind or another worked in factories, dug for victory, gave up their aluminium baths and saucepans, joined organisations and aided in any way they could. These boys from were not going to be left out; they might be too young to fight but while there were sandbags to be filled they were going to do their bit to protect their school building. Thousands of sandbags were used during World War II to protect the country and its beautiful civic buildings.

In 1939 Britain's Prime Minister Neville Chamberlain had made his announcement to the waiting people of Britain that '...this country is at war with Germany.' The country rolled up its sleeves and prepared for the inevitable. This war would be different from other wars. This time planes had the ability to fly further and carry a heavier load, and air raids were fully expected. Air raid shelters were obviously going to be needed, and shelters were built on open places across towns and cities. By the time war was declared an army of volunteers of both sexes had already been recruited to form an Air Raid Protection service. At first ARP personnel were unpaid volunteers but when war broke out in September 1939 they became paid staff. It was their job to patrol specified areas, making sure that no chinks of light broke the blackout restrictions, checking the safety of local residents, being alert for gas attacks, air raids and unexploded bombs. The exceptional work done by Air Raid Wardens in dealing with incendiaries, giving first aid to the injured, helping to rescue victims from their bombed-out properties, clearing away rubble, and a thousand and one other tasks became legendary; during the second world war nearly as many private citizens were killed as troops - and many of them were the gallant ARP wardens. At the beginning of the war Sir Anthony Eden, Secretary of State for War, appealed in a radio broadcast for men between 17 and 65 to make up a new force, the Local Defence Volunteers, to guard vulnerable points from possible Nazi attack. Within a very short time the first men were putting their names down. At first the new force had to improvise; there were no weapons to spare and men had to rely on sticks, shotguns handed in by local people, and on sheer determination. Weapons and uniforms did not become available for several months. In July the Local Defence Volunteers was renamed the Home Guard, and by the following year were a force to be reckoned with. Television programmes such as 'Dad's Army' have unfortunately associated the Home Guard with comedy, but in fact they performed much important work. The Guard posted sentries to watch for possible aircraft or parachute landings at likely spots such as disused aerodromes, golf courses on the outskirts of towns, local parks and racecourses. They manned anti-aircraft rocket guns, liaised with other units and with regular troops, set up communications and organised balloon barrages. Other preparations were hastily made. Place names and other identifying marks were obliterated to confuse the enemy about exactly where they were. Notices went up everywhere giving good advice to citizens on a number of issues. 'Keep Mum - she's not so dumb' warned people to take care what kind of information they passed on, as the person they were speaking to could be an enemy.

Older readers will remember how difficult it was to find certain items in the shops during the war; combs, soap, cosmetics, hairgrips, elastic, buttons, zips - all were virtually impossible to buy as factories that once produced these items had been turned over to war work. Stockings were in short supply, and resourceful women resorted to colouring their legs with gravy browning or with a mixture of sand and water. Beetroot juice was found to be a good substitute for lipstick.

Clothes rationing was introduced in 1941, and everyone had 66 coupons per year. Eleven coupons would buy a dress, and sixteen were needed for a coat. The number of coupons was later reduced to 40 per person. People were required to save material where they could - ladies' hemlines went up considerably, and skirts were not allowed to have lots of pleats. Some found clever ways around the regulations by using materials that were not rationed. Blackout material could be embroidered and made into blouses or skirts, and dyed sugar sacks were turned into curtains.

Transforming the world

In simple terms Edinburgh's VA TECH Elin Transformers, Edinburgh Ltd, based in Bath Road, Leith Dock, designs and builds large power transformers - the basic equipment with which power companies use to aid the actually generatation, transmission and distribution of the electricity which today we all take for granted.

In a highly competitive industry the company is a world leader. In the closing year of the 20th century this highly efficient business had achieved an annual turnover of £40 million, making the company a major player, not only in the local economy, but in that of Scotland as a whole.

Reaching back more than a century, the history of Edinburgh-based VA TECH Elin Transformers, Edinburgh mirrors the history of power generation in the United Kingdom and the world. The company's

Top left: Founder, David Bruce Peebles.
Right: Tay Works, Bonnington, Leith, the company's first electrical shop, 1898. *Below:* Official and employees at Tay Works in 1902.

success has reflected the changes that the power generation industry has risen to meet, in fuelling the UK's phenomenal industrial growth and in the demand for reliable sources of power. But in April 1999 VA Tech Elin Transformers, Edinburgh was at the centre of one of the worst industrial fires ever to occur in Scotland - the factory being razed to the ground - and that could have been the end of an already long tale.

The story of the company goes back to 1866 and to Dundee born David Bruce Peebles. A former railways engineer, Peebles had entered the gas industry in 1857 as a partner in an Edinburgh firm of gas meter manufacturers; in 1866 however, at the age of forty, he

started up in business for himself.

Bruce Peebles founded the small firm of D Bruce Peebles & Co in a workshop at Fountain-bridge where he began to make gas appliances on his own.

A decade later the firm had to move to larger premises, and in 1876 new works were built in North Leith, which Peebles named the Tay Works.

A variety of gas appliances were produced, such as gas engines and improved burners for gas lights. David Bruce Peebles foresaw the many potential uses of his gas engines but realised that to obtain the greatest benefit from the use of gas its energy should be converted into electricity which was then just beginning to have a major

impact on lives. In 1898 an electrical department was started in an existing brick building with an old unused house for an office.

The firm's first electrical dynamos were large and slow and built under conditions of strict secrecy to prevent competitors finding out what was going on. The first major order was to introduce complete electrification to the quarries near Ecclefechan in Dumfriesshire, supplying two 90 kW dynamos and a number of weather-proof motors.

Many pioneer electric lighting and power installations were undertaken in the late 1890s, with Peebles dynamos producing over 50,000 'electrical horsepower' for lighting and tramway operations by the end of the century.

Top: A general view of East Pilton Works and Offices circa 1904. ***Above left:*** *A 'highly ventilated' 140 kW gas engine, 1902.* ***Below:*** *Bruce Peebles & Co. Ltd.'s 4000 kVA transformer on a road transport truck*

By the time the founder died in 1899 at the age of 73 he had laid the foundation of an organisation which was set to grow and grow.

In 1904 the directors of what was now a limited company approved the purchase of ten acres of land at East Pilton for a new electrical works: the East Pilton Works were erected and equipped at a cost of £93,000: the gas department continued at the Tay Works, before, in 1908, becoming a separate independent company, Peebles & Co Ltd.

The first major venture at the East Pilton works was for large rotating electrical machines using designs from the Budapest firm of Ganz & Co. At the beginning German labour was imported to help, but soon the expanding industry began to attract local labour as well as men from universities and public schools from far and wide who were also attracted to this state of the art enterprise.

The most dramatic work which had caught men's imaginations at the time was the invention in 1904 of the Peeble-La Cour Motor Converter: the first order for which came from London's West Ham Corporation for 500 kW and 250 kW machines. This wonderful machine played a great part in the company's fortunes for a quarter of a century, during which time equipment capable in total of producing nearly a million kW would be supplied for service all over the world.

Meanwhile no contract was too large - in 1904 1,500 kW generators were supplied to the Upper Boat power station in South Wales, whilst in 1906 the company completed Britain's first large hydro-electric project - the Snowdon Scheme - including tunnelling and installing transmission lines. Electrification of tramways in places as far apart as Sunderland and Shanghai and Athens and Colwyn Bay were successfully undertaken. Less happily the building of electric locomotives for the ill-fated South Snowdon narrow gauge railway, which was abandoned in 1908, caused financial difficulties and lead to a period of retrenchment which lasted until the outbreak of the Great War.

During the 1914-18 war the company made high explosive shells, hydro-phones for submarine detection, gun mountings and aircraft parts.

Top left: A 130-ton 75,000 kVA Generator Transformer, one of two built in 1949 for Portobello Power Station. Above right: With just one inch clearance from the top of the Welding Shop a huge tank for a 73,000 kVA Transformer moves out the first stage of its journey to London. Right: The second of two 120 MVA 275 kV auto-transformer set out on its way to the south of Scotland Electricity Board's Sub-Station at Clyde Mill, Glasgow.

by which time the company was more than ready to do its bit.

Early in 1939, even before the declaration of war with Hitler's Germany, the company's technical resources had been mobilised by Government orders for anti-aircraft, tank and emergency electrical equipment. Now with war actually declared black out and camouflage measures were taken and air-raid shelters built.

Emergency mobile electrical plant was supplied for powering essential services in Britain's blitzed cities. Contrasting with the high voltage transformers for the National Grid many small ones, totalling 75,000 by 1945, were also made for mobile radio transmitters.

New equipment to combat new enemy devices were designed, novel inventions such as those used as counter-measures against magnetic mines (de-gaussing and consequent compass correction of ships) and the

A short-lived post war boom saw a surge in sales, not least in very large hydro-electric generators destined for New Zealand. In the late 1920s however a trade slump saw the company at its lowest ebb. Not until 1932 did there begin a period of modernisation in a programme designed to make the company's electrical department one of the most up-to-date in the country. The work of modernisation continued until the outbreak of the second world war in 1939

*Top and above left: King George VI, Queen Elizabeth, the late Queen Mother, and Queen Elizabeth II (the then) Princess Elizabeth made two visits to East Pilton Works in 1942 and 1944. **Below:** Electric motors on view at an exhibition.*

acoustic mine; minesweeping equipment was also supplied to the Royal Navy throughout the war.

Powerful mobile searchlights and intricate equipment for the electrical control of anti-aircraft guns were manufactured, whilst weapons made at East Pilton included a multiple rocket projector and the famous 'PIAT' mortar. So successful was this Portable Infantry Anti-Tank gun that a special department was set up for it, most of the workers being women.

The high point of the company's war effort however came with the order for 'Whales' - pontoons for the famous Mulberry harbours. Though the delivery time was incredibly short Bruce Peebles workers had this Top Secret order fabricated in time for D-day, in the aftermath of which the floating Mulberry harbours would pay such a vital part in keeping supplies flowing to the advancing Allied forces.

Emergency bridge parts were also constructed and sent overseas. The Allied advance encountered roads strewn with metal wreckage strewn by the enemy: Bruce

Peebles electromagnets, fitted in front of bulldozers, helped to clear the routes.

Recognition of the company's contribution to the war effort was made when King George VI and Queen Elizabeth visited the works in 1942 and in 1944, on the second occasion they were accompanied by the then Princess Elizabeth.

Following the war's end the company would revert to its normal peacetime activities. And happily, unlike the

Top left: *A 14,000 kVA Generator built in 1953 for the Niingen Power Station, Norway.* **Above:** *A 1960s interior of the heavy machine shop and light machine section on the right.* **Left:** *A birds eye view of East Pilton Works in 1958.* **Below:** *Fitters at work on a 64-inch magnet for Mitchell Engineering, Glasgow, 1958.*

Meanwhile for staff in the 1950s many social and recreational interests were catered for by the company's Social and Sports Club. Another useful amenity was a Works Library which contained a wide selection of technical, general interest, fiction and reference books

1920s, the post war boom would not peter out in economic depression. Pre-war the company had already played an important role in the electrification of the Southern Region of British railways, now a high point of the post war years from 1947 to 1954 would be the company's role in what was then one of the most important railway engineering achievements of the times - the electrification of the Manchester - Sheffield railway line which marked the first application in Britain of 1,500 volts DC to mainline railway work. Bruce Peebles rectifier sub-station equipment was used exclusively on the railway line for the conversion of the 33,000 volt AC supply to 1,500 volts DC for delivery to the overhead conductor system.

No doubt the library was well used by apprentices. Elsewhere a comprehensive Welfare Service was provided by the company, a benefit which included a Medical Service as well as a branch of the St John's Ambulance Corps; and whilst the well-used staff canteen catered for employees' physical needs their spiritual welfare was catered for by a visiting

Industrial Chaplain. Nor was care of the elderly former staff overlooked. In 1950 the Wardie Men's Club for retired employees was formed by the Industrial Chaplain the Reverend James Rennie and Company Secretary WM McKenzie.

Top, both pictures: *Staff photographs 1961.*
Right: *A 60 MVA Synchronous Condenser now called Synchronous Compensator, the largest made by BP in the 1960s.* ***Below:*** *Two MVA Single Phase Electrification Transformers at Strathleven, 1960s.*

In 1961 the Bruce Peebles Industries Group of companies was created as a result of a merger of a number of companies in the United Kingdom, each of which had been established for many years. The Group's largest factory however would remain that in Edinburgh.

By the late 1960s Bruce Peebles Industries was employing some 3,000 people in several factories in Scotland. Overseas the Group had subsidiaries in Australia, South Africa and Canada with exports being made to every part of the globe, progress which had its culmination in the company gaining the Queen's Award for Export in 1974.

Nor was that the last award: in 1989 what was now Peebles Transformers Ltd was acquired by Rolls Royce, two years later a second Queen's award for Export was gained.

In 1998 Peebles Transformers was acquired by VA Technolgie AG, an engineering Group based in Austria and active world-wide as a system supplier in metallurgical engineering, energy and environmental engineering and services. The following year however the majority of the entire Peebles site was destroyed by fire.

On 12th April 1999 the company gained the unenviable record for being the centre of one of the most devastating industrial fires in Scotland's history.

The fire had spread with almost unbelievable ferocity, and afterwards the factory looked as if it had been literally bombed as a result of the igniting gas inside the plant causing massive explosions.

The facts speak for themselves: at the height of the blaze smoke could be seen from 55 miles away, and at its peak the temperatures within the factory were as high as those found within a blast furnace.

Top right and above: *The Queen and the Duke of Edinburgh visit East Pilton Works, May 1969.*
Far left: *1999 saw one of the worst industrial fires ever to occur in Scotland at VA TECH Peebles Transformers factory.*
Left: *A 132kV Grid Transformer installed in Scotland over 60 years ago, and still in service.*

Undaunted the company's managers recovered and within days the parent company had given the go-ahead to build the most modern engineering plant ever built in Scotland - in the process securing the jobs of most of the company's workers.

A brand new state of the art factory was opened at a new site in Leith Dock in August 2000. The following year the world's largest 400kV 'quadrature booster' passed its factory test and was dispatched to its end user, the UK's National Grid Co.

The new factory employs some 300 people and concentrates on the design and manufacture of large power transformers including three phase and single phase Generator Step Up and Transmission transformers, Phase Shifters and those large Quadrature Boosters.

VA TECH Elin Transformers, Edinburgh Ltd, as the company is now known, is today part of VA TECH's Transmission and Distribution business - and part of a global transformer group which has eight other manufacturing facilities around the world. David Bruce Peebles would surely have been both astonished and delighted to see how his once small enterprise had developed since it started out in 1866.

*Top left: Autotransformers and Reactors on test for a Zimbabwe project. **Above left:** A 2000 MVA 400kV Quadrature Booster for the UK National Grid Company. **Below:** VA TECH Elin Transformers, Edinburgh new state-of-the-art factory at the Port of Leith, completed in 2000.*

Yet the fire that so devastated the Pilton factory turned out to have had a simple cause.

During the post-fire investigation it emerged that the cause of the blaze was a failed capacitor located outside the factory.

Capacitors are about the size of a television set and are filled with oil. One had ruptured and set a spark that moved through the factory wall and ignited materials stored inside the plant. Within an hour the entire factory was ablaze, and within three hours it was clear that all that the company would be left with was a ruin.

Fortunately evacuation procedures went smoothly, and no one was harmed. The enormity of the disaster was reflected however in the fact that the no fewer then 17 fire crews attended the blaze, whilst the fire brigade would maintain a presence on site for no less than six weeks!

Events & Occasions

What a magnificent sight to see George VI and Queen Elizabeth, subsequently the much loved 'Queen Mum', making their state entry to Edinburgh in July 1937. Sadly in this photo the King's features are obscured behind a coach lamp, but we get a fine view of his Queen. Heading east along Princes Street, past the Scott Monument with Edinburgh Castle in the background, the crowds surge forward on both side of the carriageway to get a glimpse of their new sovereign. Few nations if any can compete with the Scots when it comes to pomp and pageantry and this occasion was one to match the best. There was a great surge of sympathy for the shy, sensitive George who never really wanted to be king. The pressure of the job would drive him to an early grave in 1952, though not before he and Queen Elizabeth had won the hearts of the nation in the darkest days of the second world war, never flinching from doing their duty. It is said that George VI actually made the modern monarchy: that may be an overstatement or at least an over simplification. Certainly his elder brother now the Duke of Windsor had brought the monarchy into some disrepute, though hardly as much as his grandfather Edward VII. What King George and Queen Elizabeth however did achieve was turning the Royal family into a family in which the whole nation could share. Even though hard line republicans may have been unimpressed, the majority have remained loyal to the idea of the monarchy.

What pomp and splendour accompany the King and Queen as their procession makes its way through the streets of Edinburgh, amidst flying banners whilst flanked by kilted soldiers - and running cameramen eager to get the best snap of the day for their newspaper or magazine. The paparazzi are not a new invention! This spectacular view looking west along Princes street has been taken by a cameraman perched high on the Scott Monument, and what a splendid and memorable sight it surely was for everyone present on that glorious July day in 1937 as George VI, Queen Elizabeth and their entourage descended on Scotland's capital. The crowds line the roadside ten and twenty deep to catch a glimpse of their new sovereign, whilst a standard-bearer soldier dips his colours as the royal carriage passes by. Soldiers who make their oath of allegiance to the sovereign look on with pride. They may, however, have also been feeling some trepidation about what the immediate future had in store for them. Over on the continent Herr Hitler had already been the Fuhrer or 'leader' of Germany for three years; he had already begun rearming as well as training his Condor Legion by loaning it to General Franco during the Spanish Civil War. In 1937 peace was still possible, however older hands warned that in their view the peace treaty signed with Germany after the first world war had been too lenient, and that the Germans should have been crushed absolutely, to make the possibility of another German war quite impossible.

Never mind the Americans with their 4th July celebrations, this is 7th July 1937 and the occasion for this party in Newton Street is the coronation of George VI and his state visit to the capital city of Scotland. Never mind the great depression which gave the decade the name the hungry thirties, this at least was one day to forgot our woes and have a day to remember. In East Princes Street Gardens a fabulous flower display proclaimed George Rex 1937 whilst at Saughton a firework display picked out in vivid flame the outlines of the King and Queen in addition to those of the young Princesses, Elizabeth and Margaret Rose. The youngsters pictured here enjoying themselves in Newton Street will all be pensioners now, but how may of them still cherish fond memories of this golden day? Some youngsters there that day however may find their memories somewhat muddled: King Edward VIII had only ascended to the throne in January 1936 but had abdicated within less than a year to make his life with the American divorcee Wallace Simpson. Edward's younger brother George became king on December 10th 1936 with the result that there had been three kings on the throne during a single year. With such a bewildering turn of events who would be surprised to find that some schoolchildren were slightly puzzled by it all. But if you didn't understand it at least you could enjoy it. This would be the last time for public rejoicing before the outbreak of the second world war - best make the most of it whilst one could.

By courtesy of Edinburgh City Libraries

By courtesy of Edinburgh City Libraries

WELCOME.

By courtesy of Edinburgh City Libraries

Events of the 1930s

WHAT'S ON?
In this heyday of the cinema, horrified audiences were left gasping at the sight of Fay Wray in the clutches of the giant ape in the film 'King Kong', released in 1933. Very different but just as gripping was the gutsy 1939 American Civil War romance 'Gone with the Wind'. Gable's parting words, 'Frankly, my dear, I don't give a damn' went down in history.

GETTING AROUND
At the beginning of the decade many believed that the airship was the transport of the future. The R101 airship, however, loaded with thousands of cubic metres of hydrogen, crashed in France on its maiden flight in 1930. Forty-eight passengers and crew lost their lives. In 1937 the Hindenburg burst into flames - the entire disaster caught on camera and described by a distraught reporter. The days of the airship were numbered.

SPORTING CHANCE
The black American Jesse Owens won a brilliant four world records in the 1936 Olympic Games in Berlin, thumbing the nose to Adolf Hitler's dreams of Aryan superiority. In a petty display Hitler walked out of the stadium and 'took his bat home'; later he refused to have his photograph taken with the victorious Owens.

By courtesy of Edinburgh City Libraries

Above: Holyrood Palace or the Palace of Holyrood-house is the setting for this Royal Garden Party being held on 7th July 1937 during the state visit of the newly crowned George VI and Queen Elizabeth. For admirals of the Royal Navy, generals in the army and senior officers of the RAF as well as other important dignitaries this is an opportunity to get close to the fount of all authority. Yet, although this is an important occasion for VIPs, others less exalted such as girl guides and boy scouts also have the opportunity to be near their sovereign, and perhaps for them the occasion is even more awe inspiring than for those more used to such high flown circles. The Palace itself of course would be indifferent to all such events having seen everything worth seeing in its long life. Holyrood Abbey dates back to 1128 and the reign of King David I. James VI created the palace in 1501 from a guesthouse attached to Holyrood Abbey. Since then the palace has housed James V, as well as Mary Queen of Scots who spent six eventful years living within its walls during which time she married both Darnley and Bothwell, in addition to witnessing the murder of he secretary Rizzio and debating theology with the redoubtable John Knox. James VI was the last permanent royal resident although Bonnie Prince Charlie did stay here briefly in 1745. Largely neglected thereafter the palace was happily brought back from decay following the visit of George IV to Scotland in 1822 and rose to further eminence during the reign of Queen Victoria.

It's the junction of Marchmont Road and Melville Drive. The date is June 1953, so why are all these crowds gathered here? Is it to celebrate KDM McGregor Provision Merchants? No of course not, the crowds have gathered to see that white gloved lady in the back of the limousine: Queen Elizabeth II. (or Elizabeth the first for those who want to argue the point). The Queen had been crowned in Westminster Abbey on 2 June and was now making her Royal Progress through her northern kingdom. What were the members of this flag-waving crowd thinking one wonders? Some readers may actually have been in this scene and recognise themselves. Most folk were filled with optimism, and enchanted by a new and above all, young monarch. Not since Queen Victoria ascended the throne had the country been granted so young a monarch, let alone a young Queen. Many in the crowd would still easily remember the final years of Queen Victoria's long reign and recall her remarkable affection for Scotland. That the new Queen was herself married to Prince Phillip who had taken the title Duke of Edinburgh was an indication that Queen Victoria's high regard and affection for the north would continue to burn fiercely in the heart of her young successor. More than fifty years on that hope has been realised with Her Majesty still travelling north every year to spend time in Scotland.

Tuesday the 2nd of May 1945 was not the end of the second world war, which was still being waged in the Far East against Japan; but it was the end of the war against Germany. The ending of European hostilities was celebrated by the whole nation as VE Day - Victory in Europe. Throughout Britain street parties were held to mark the momentous good news. Typical of such parties is that pictured here at Kemp place in the Stockbridge Colonies. Under the lion of Scotland and many other flags folk are sitting down for an outdoor meal to mark the triumph of Allied forces over the tyranny of Hitler and his Nazis. For many sat around the tables, which have been carried out in the street, it marks a new beginning, a period of hope after years of despair, the promise of full stomachs after years of rationing and the end of fear after six years of terror. For others present it is a time to look forward to the return of loved ones, some of whom were captured years earlier on the retreat to Dunkirk. For others it is a time for quiet tears away from the festivities, a time to remember those loved ones who will never return. For youngsters however, many of whom had no memories of a time without war, it was simply a time to enjoy oneself, to eat food that had been hoarded against this great day, to gorge, if only for a single day, on cakes and jellies, buns and pies. And perhaps also to ask questions like 'When will we get some of those bananas you're always talking about grandad?'

Any reader who recalls this tranquil scene looking east along Princes Street would need to be well in to their eighties. The photograph was taken sometime around 1920 and the relative absence of traffic is something of a shock to those familiar with today's nose to tail traffic. These were the days when it was not only possible to park your car on the street but to do so outside the actual shop one wanted to visit. In 1920 few people owned a car of their own, indeed there will still plenty of horses and carts about, though in this scene the small wheeled vehicle in the foreground loaded with baskets is having to rely on manpower to pull it along past Lugton's boot maker's shop. Despite the cheerfulness

Shopping spree

of the scene the year 1920 was not a particularly happy one for Scotland. There was good news and bad news. The good news was that a peace treaty had finally been signed which finally drew a formal line under the first world war. The bad news for Scottish industry was that shares in Scottish distilleries were badly hit when the USA, one of the largest markets for whisky, had introduced prohibition. Both peace treaty and prohibition would prove to be poison chalices: the unfair terms imposed on Germany would lead to the rise of the Nazis led by Adolph Hitler whilst Americans' continuing, though now illegal, demand for alcohol would fuel black market gangsterism personified by Chicago mobster Al Capone.

West End Princes Street pictured from the Caledonian Hotel offers a fine vista on this sunny afternoon in 1950. The flat topped trams of earlier years have been partly replaced by more modern looking vehicles. The open platform bus pictured here is now long gone too - in the interests of safety. How many readers however recall chasing after a missed bus and just managing to leap aboard as the vehicle picked up speed - and how many recall hopping off at a location more convenient than the bus stop as the driver slowed to negotiate a corner? Come to that how many middle aged daredevils overestimating their agility, tried the same stunt and ended up with a broken leg? Such buses were of course not only dangerous and draughty but they were also uneconomic since they required a conductor as well as a driver. Meanwhile on this gloriously warm day thousands of shoppers have got off the buses and trams and are lining the pavements to walk along the pavement. The shopkeepers have put out their awnings to stop the bright sunshine fading the goods in the windows. Only one thing suggests that the day my not be quite as hot as it looks: the smoke billowing from a chimney on the far left. Though many readers will feel a pang of nostalgia when gazing at this scene in truth few of us can regret the loss of coal fires and smoking chimneys which played havoc with clean washing and delicate lungs.

Beyond doubt the most distinctive store along Edinburgh's Princes Street is Jenners, a store which generations of Edinburgh citizens have grown to love, and which has in turn grown with that affection. This photo taken in 1966 shows Jenners growing a little more with a new extension being constructed on the western side of the older building. The original, and earlier, Jenner and Kennington store had opened in 1838 and for more than 50 years it was essentially a ladies fashion store. On 26th November 1892 a fire broke out in the basement, the ensuing conflagration destroyed not only the original store but also the dormitories, which accommodated some 120 out of town workers. Happily the workers surviced, but the store was beyond saving. The building we know today and pictured here, was completed within three years of the famous fire. Built of Aberdeen granite and yellow freestone the 'wondrous renaissance compilation' was designed by W Hamilton Beattie and, at the suggestion of Charles Jenner, echoed Oxford's Bodleian library. On its opening day in 1895 25,000 passed through its doors. Those who have lived in Edinburgh all their lives probably rarely if ever cast their eyes upward to examine this extraordinary building above street level, but to do so certainly pays dividends. Though the whole building is ornate its upper storey is truly remarkable, a tribute to the stonemasons art - something which due to cost and changing taste is now most unlikely ever to be repeated.

Events of the 1950s

SCIENCE AND DISCOVERY

DNA (deoxyribonucleic acid) was first defined as long ago as 1953, and the effects have been far-reaching. The key discovery was developed over the following years and today DNA fingerprinting has become an accepted part of life. Genetic diseases such as haemophilia and cystic fibrosis have been identified. Criminals are continually detected and brought to justice. Biological drugs have been developed. More controversially, drought and disease-resistant plants have been engineered - and Dolly the sheep has been produced.

MELODY MAKERS

Few teenage girls could resist the blatant sex-appeal of 'Elvis the Pelvis', though their parents were scandalised at the moody Presley's provocatively gyrating hips. The singer took America and Britain by storm with such hits as 'Jailhouse Rock', 'All Shook Up' and 'Blue Suede Shoes'. The rhythms of Bill Haley and his Comets, Buddy Holly, Chuck Berry, and Roy Orbison (who had a phenomenal three-octave voice) turned the 1950s into the Rock 'n' Roll years.

INVENTION AND TECHNOLOGY

Until the late 1950s you did not carry radios around with you. Radios were listened to at home, plugged into a mains socket in every average sitting room. Japan was in the forefront of electronic developments even then, and in 1957 the Japanese company Sony introduced the world's very first all-transistor radio - an item of new technology that was small enough to fit into your pocket. The major consumer product caught on fast - particularly with teenage listeners.

Below: On 23rd June 1953 cheering crowds had greeted the Queen and Prince Philip as they made a royal progress through the streets of Edinburgh, travelling in an open horse-drawn carriage. That was only the start of a busy week for the young royal couple. One of the highlights of their stay would be their attendance at the 'Masque of Edinburgh' historical pageant held at Usher hall four days later. No sooner had the Coronation been celebrated in London on June 2nd than it was time for Scotland to prepare for the state visit of Queen Elizabeth II and the Duke of Edinburgh. They took up residence at Holyroodhouse from the 23rd to the 29th of June. Edinburgh was decked out for a party; a lot of interest was aroused at the innovative decorations to be seen at Jenners on Princes Street, decorations captured here for all time by an impressed cameraman. The famous Princes Street store had managed to come up with a solution to the problem of finding something new to put on show. Some may have thought that the building was already ornate enough, but Jenners improved on it. Not only was the whole building lavishly decorated with banners, shields and flags, but what really caught the public's eye was the series of replicas of the 'Queen's Beasts' placed between upper parts of the ground floor windows. Lions, griffins and unicorns were featured emblazoned in full heraldic colour. Between each pair of beasts there were royal coat-of-arms.

Right: This photograph of Jenners taken in the early 1950s features Edinburgh's wonderful old trams. The trams are long gone but Jenners endures. Nobody knows if Charles Jenner and his friend Charles Kennington had a winning day at the Musselburgh Races in 1837; in one sense however they certainly did - though it can't have seemed like that at the time. They got the sack for unauthorised absence from work, an event which naturally set them wondering what to do next. The idea they produced was to turn out a winner: they would open a shop together. Eight months later that shop, Kennington and Jenner, opened on the corner of Princes Street and South St David Street, a business with the declared aim of providing 'every prevailing British and Parisian fashion in Silks, Shawls, Fancy Dresses, Linen, Drapery and Haberdashery'. From that small if ambitious start arose the world-famous department store of Jenners, an Edinburgh landmark selling all that was originally promised - and much more. Charles Kennington and Charles Jenner worked long hours, the latter sometimes sleeping overnight in the shop on a mat behind the counter. By 1860 several shops had been added to the original premises. Jenner continued alone when his partner died in 1863. Jenner himself died in 1895 shortly before the grand opening of the present building, an architectural delight featuring the lovely caryatids - a tribute to the women whom Jenner said metaphorically were 'the support of the house' and who would in future do so quite literally.

Above: No the car on the left is not about to run down
the pedestrians in this bus queue, nor is it about to
crash head on into the No 10 bus - it's simply parked, a
much missed privilege by motorists who today often
spend as much time looking for somewhere to leave
their vehicles as they do on the journey itself. The
cameraman has captured no fewer than four Edinburgh
Corporation buses making their way along Lothian Road
in 1958. On the face of it this is a recognisably modern
scene and yet one feature jumps out to point unmistak-
ably to the past: though the quality of Scotland's fine
whiskies may be still be advertised on anything from
street hoardings to buses tobacco advertising has all but
gone. Those who enjoy both a glass of whisky and a
cigarette will feel a pang of nostalgia as the read the
words 'Enjoy another packet of Capstan - they're
blended better'. This was still the age when smokers
could smoke in peace and without the annoying
warnings that smoking might be unhealthy. Many more
men still smoked pipes, whilst tipped cigarettes were
still seen as a little effeminate - even if they did away
with the problem of lips sticking to the cigarette paper
and shreds of tobacco ending up on your tongue. This
was still the age when smoking was perfectly acceptable
on the upper deck of buses, and even cinemas thought-
fully provide ashtrays between the backs of seats. How
many readers, we wonder, enjoyed their first illicit
Woodbine on the back row of the cinema?

It's quarter past three in the afternoon on Princes Street, but for the trams in the centre of this scene its one minute to midnight. Yes 1956 was the last year Edinburgh folk would have the chance to take a ride on their beloved trams, though being practical as well as sentimental, the city's citizen's recognised the need for progress. And indeed many would observe that for all that they liked the trams, they didn't care overmuch for the overhead cables which cross-crossed the skies and made all too convenient perches for resting birds who were all too keen to drop sudden messages from on high and onto the coats and jackets of unwary pedestrians. In this scene the whole southern side of Princes Street has been cordoned off and traffic is being directed by a white-sleeved policeman onto the northern carriageway. Despite the doubling up of traffic on the far side of the road the scene appears remarkably uncongested: try pulling a stunt like this in the 21st century and the city would be grid-locked. On the right of the picture are the magnificent Italianate-style offices of the Life Association of Scotland. This dominating building is typical of Edinburgh's Victorian heritage, and indeed of Britain's Victorian era when the Pax Britannica echoed the imperial Pax Romana of two thousand years earlier. Neo-classical architecture abounded as Britain saw itself as the new Rome and architects responded by designing classically styled buildings to reflect that imperial presumption.

Below: 'What's 6d mean Dad?' Youngsters today may know what pounds are, but ask them about shillings, sixpences and three-penny bits and they're apt to look a little blank. As can be seen on the advert for the Monster Carnival just sixpence (go on, explain to them: it's 2 1/2 p in decimal currency) will gain one admission to the event which seems to be linked with the circus coming to town. This view is taken from Waverly Bridge looking up towards Princes Street. The date as witnessed by the trams still plying their route is the early 1950s when there were still 240 real pennies in a pound and sixpence could buy a fair bit of fun. In those days half a crown (12 1/2p) was enough to pay for a tram ride into the city, a visit to the cinema, buy enough beer to sink a ship, get a fish and chip supper on the way home and still have enough change left over to buy a three piece suit and a pair of boots - well almost! As for this scene it remains readily identifiable even half a century on, though the corner in the foreground has been redeveloped as one of Edinburgh's most modern shopping centres. A 1950s passenger emerging from Waverley Station today would not feel in the least disoriented, even if the trams have long since disappeared to be replaced by buses whose fares would take a 1950s traveller's breath away.

Right: South Bridge in 1958 presents a remarkably traffic free scene. Well, almost traffic free, with barely half a dozen cars in sight. Today, even an early Sunday morning would not be so relatively free from cars. Double yellow lines the scourge of the modern motorist are still several years in the future, though white line man has already put

in an appearance to mark out the bus stops. Though the dearth of traffic gives the scene an authentic period feel it is however the ladies' fashions which really give the game away. Take a close look at those hemlines and you'll know for sure that this is a photograph taken just prior to the swinging sixties, when hemlines shot suddenly skyward to the delight of young men and to the despair of anxious fathers. The late 1950s were a time of soaring hope after a long period of post-war austerity. Unemployment was at an all time low and wages were rising rapidly. Prime Minster Harold Macmillan observed in a speech made in 1957 that the British people had never had it so good. And he was right, though opposition leaders, not unnaturally, challenged his opinion. Older folk of course knew better too: hadn't they lived through the post war boom of the early 1920s?, only to see that brief flash of prosperity wither to nothing in the great depression of the 1930s. 'The 1960s will be just like the 1930s with millions unemployed' the doomsayers predicted.

Above right: Though it may be hard to believe it does sometimes rain in Edinburgh. Just to prove it here's a picture taken on a wet afternoon in 1955. Though the eye is immediately caught by the signs for the Royal British Hotel its entrance is on the other side of the building; what we are

treated to here is Burton's Tailor and Elliott's bookshop. Just for once Burton's doesn't have a dance hall or snooker hall above it - perhaps the only Burton's branch in the country not offering such features. Alongside Woolworth's and Marks and Spencer's, Montague Burton was one to the very first 'multiples' to be a familiar name in almost every high street. Today almost every shop is part of a large chain. On the right is the old Palace Picture House featuring Danny Kaye's 1952 film Hans Christian Anderson. Born David Daniel Kaminsky in Brooklyn in 1913, Danny Kaye was the son of an immigrant Russian tailor and would become one of the world's best-loved entertainers. Throughout his career he starred in seventeen movies, including The Kid From Broadway (1946), The Secret Life of Walter Mitty (1947), the Inspector General (1949) and the unforgettable The Court Jester (1956) in which court jester Kaye, displays the vocal talents which made him famous when he says simply, "The pellet with the poison's in the vessel with the pestle, the chalice from the palace has the brew that is true" Kaye died of a heart attack in Los Angeles, California in 1987.

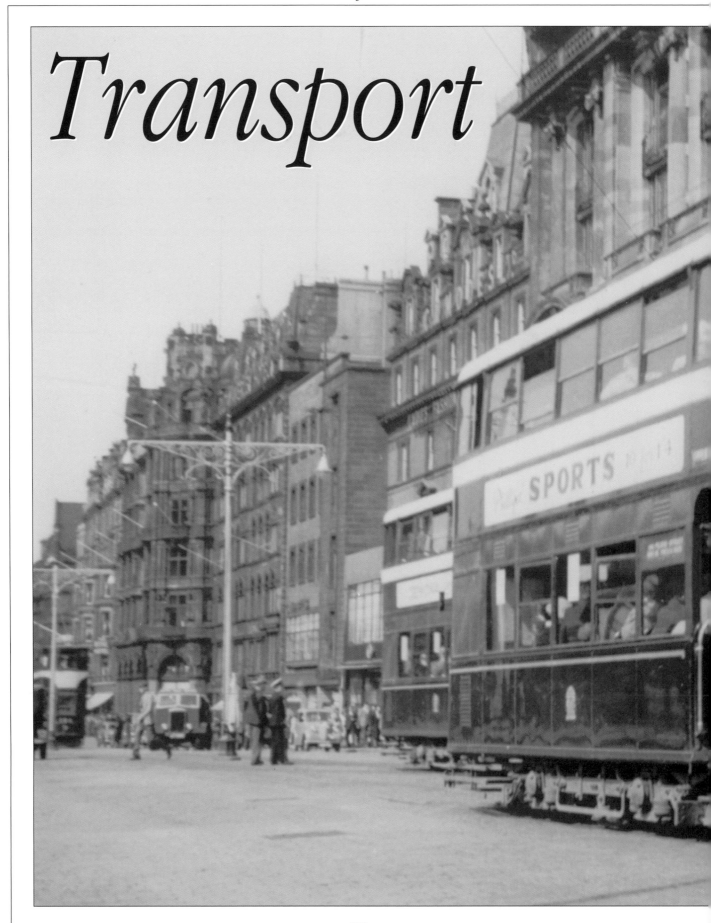

Transport

In 1952 when tram number 247 was captured on film trams still outnumbered Edinburgh's buses. That year however the tram system began its slide into oblivion. Four years later Edinburgh's tramway system with its iron rails set in the roadway and its overhead electric cables had disappeared entirely. The distinctive maroon and white livery would quickly become just a distant memory for the generations which had been brought up to be familiar with the whine an rattle of the tramcars as they gathered speed and the driver's low-pitched bell warning folk to get out of the way. Having previously had its unusual and unreliable cable system since 1888 that older system had been completely replaced by the more orthodox, and more reliable system by 1923. Edinburgh's last tram would make its final journey to the Shrubhill depot on 16th November 1956. Though thousands came out to watch that final historic journey for many others of far more concern was the Suez Crisis which that same day had witnessed Egypt block the canal by sinking no fewer than 49 ships in its waters following the invasion of Egypt by British, French and Israeli forces. The Suez Crisis would end in the political humiliation of Britain and France by the USA which refused to support the enterprise. The consequence would be a loss of national prestige, but also the loss of the lives of Scottish servicemen - men who gave up their lives for their country yet who would never receive official recognition in the form of a war memorial.

By courtesy of Edinburgh City Libraries

By courtesy of Edinburgh City Libraries

Above: It's a quarter past one on 30th January 1954. Tram no 302 is waiting outside Morningside Road Station. What might it be that has so excited our cameraman that he has gone out in the cold and snow to capture the scene for generations yet to come? The answer is not the photographer's obsessive interest in Bernard's Ales and Stouts advertised on the side of this tram but in the tram itself. This is the Last Day. On the penultimate day of January 1954 tram number 302 was the very last to run on route no 28 to Morningside Road railway station. Edinburgh's other trams would take a little longer to disappear entirely but their death warrant had already been signed: it would be slow death by a thousand cuts. Future generations would have to visit museums to discover what it was like to travel as their parents and grandparents had once done inside these grand old vehicles. Or perhaps they might go all the way to Blackpool to experience the only 'authentic' tramway still in daily use in Britain. One vintage Edinburgh tram did in fact make an historic visit to Blackpool as part of a vintage tram festival, though sadly it burnt out its motors before it was realised that Blackpool's voltage was significantly higher than that used by Edinburgh! Whilst proposals for a new modern tramway system continue to be considered sleek new trams can never be a substitute for the real thing pictured here.

Below: Tramcar no. 328 heads for Granton between two Trams Only signs, themselves indicative of early traffic management schemes which would in later decades lead to bus and cycle lanes. The lady in the centre of the scene looks surprised to be having her picture taken. She probably is surprised, but she can console herself with the knowledge that at least she was wearing a hat. 'Get ahead get a hat' was a clever advising slogan coined several years after this photograph was taken: in the early 1950s however no clever jingles or exhortations were needed to encourage folk to cover their heads: few self respecting men or women felt fully dressed without a hat. These days, except on formal occasions such as weddings, or when cold weather makes a hat a necessity, few of us bother with a hat. The reasons for that change are many, though no doubt include expecting to have heating everywhere whether in shops or in cars. Readers old enough to remember the 1950s however, will have memories of relatives and neighbours whom they can never, ever, recall seeing without a hat. Today only the armed forces seem to have preserved their headgear unscathed by the passage of time; other occupations such as postmen, bus drivers, bus conductors (whatever happened to bus conductors?) and railway staff all seem to have lost their once distinctive hats over the passing decades.

By courtesy of Edinburgh City Libraries

By courtesy of Edinburgh City Libraries

Above: Outside Binns department store it's five past four in the afternoon in the year 1952. When the photographer took this picture of Edinburgh tramcar number 337 it was on its way to Granton via George Street, but all to soon it was be on its way into the history books. An even earlier system of tramways had already long since disappeared: Edinburgh's cable-powered tram system. The earlier ill-fated cable system had ceased to exist in the early 1920s having been plagued by technical problems. Wear and tear badly affected the underground cable and pulley system. The 26 mile long cable system used just seven long cables, and when one broke down every tram attached to that cable came to a stop: the longest underground cable was 34,410 feet long and weighed in at an incredible 55 tones. The cable system was never truly very good,

the fastest speed was a mere 12 miles per hour, and only 8 miles per hour along its slowest stretch, a speed hardly faster than the horse trams which it had replaced in 1907. By then the future had already arrived. The first electrified tramlines had opened in Leith in November 1905. Four years later the Leith system was complete and would be a continuous reminder for neighbouring Edinburgh that the corporation had made the wrong choice. Passengers on these trams however were unlikely to be spending much time pondering on the history of public transport in the city; in 1952 the news of the day was the death of King George VI and the accession to the throne of the young Princess Elizabeth, ushering in what was promised to be a new Elizabethan age.

Below: Buses always come in threes, but if this photograph taken on Princes Street in April 1956 is to be believed Edinburgh's trams once came by the dozen. Sadly this was a scene which would never be repeated: the tram system was winding down. Thousands watched the last tram make its final journey to Shrubhill Depot on November 16th 1956. Edinburgh's first trams were horse-powered and began their operations in 1871. The application of artificial power began in 1888, the year which saw Edinburgh adopt an unusual system in which trams were pulled by steam driven cables which ran down the centre of the tracks. The steam powered cable system was not fully converted to a more orthodox electric system until 1923. To Edinburgh-born writer and broadcaster Ludovic Kennedy the nostalgia invoked by the trams of his childhood lay simply in the sounds they made, 'the whine and the rattle as they gathered speed, the driver's low-pitched bell to shoo people out of the way'. Readers whose memories extend beyond 1956 may also be whisked back to their childhood by the sight of these fine old vehicles whose distinctive maroon and white livery once dominated the city streets. They might bring back recollections of smoking Woodbines 'Wild 'uns' on the top deck, or of trying to guess if you were near your stop on cold wet nights when the condensation ran down the inside of the windows and the dim gas lights made it difficult to work out where you were.

Bird's eye view

ere we are looking west along Princes Street on a fine summer's morning in the early 1960s. At first glance, save for the road vehicles, the scene has been virtually unchanged for a century. Indeed the view to the left, with Edinburgh castle watching over the New Town, has not changed for far longer. Behind the Obelisk on the left is North Bridge whilst right in the centre of the picture is the clock tower of what was then still the North British Hotel. The 160 foot tall tower with its clock always kept a couple of minutes fast had long been an Edinburgh landmark. Sold in 1981 the building reopened ten years later as the Balmoral Hotel. To the right of the scene is the distinctive dome. the Register House home of the Scottish Record Office built between 1774 and 1827 from designs drawn up by Robert Adam. In the distance all along the north side of Princes Street sunblinds can be seen, pulled out against the noonday glare protecting the shop window displays from fading in the strong light. And on the street itself, how things have changed: just look at the line of parked cars with not a traffic warden in sight; meanwhile doesn't the sight of those buses with open platforms at the rear take you back to the days when you could still get on a bus you had just missed by running fast and risking life and limb leap to aboard the moving vehicle?

This bird's eye view from high above North Bridge and Waverley Station was taken in 1947. The scene is bisected by the North Bridge with the North British Hotel just to the left, whilst to the right can be seen the curve of Leith Street making its way northwards. Looking down at this busy scene it's hard to imagine that in the now distant past the New Town simply did not exist, the Nor' Loch filled the valley now occupied by railways and gardens whilst Old Town was the only town. In this scene New Town actually fills this view. In 1766 Edinburgh announced a competition to design an extension to the city - an extension which would become New Town north of the Nor Loch. The competition was won by 23-year-old James Craig, an unknown self-taught architect whose plan was for the main axis of the town to be George Street. The idea was for houses to be built only on one side of Princes and Queens Streets in order to ensure that their occupants would enjoy views of the castle and Old Town, in the former case and of the Firth of Forth in the latter. Squares, parks and terraces continued to be built in New Town during the next 50 years, much of it in the neoclassical style for which Edinburgh is famous. In 1995 both Old Town and New Town, with its unique collection of Georgian architecture, were declared a World Heritage Site by UNESCO.

Events of the 1960s

MELODY MAKERS

The 1960s: those were the days when the talented blues guitarist Jimi Hendrix shot to rock stardom, a youthful Cliff Richard charmed the nation with his 'Congratulations' and Sandie Shaw won the Eurovision Song Contest for Britain with 'Puppet on a String'. It was the combined musical talents of a group of outrageous working-class Liverpool lads, however, who formed the Beatles and took the world by storm with music that ranged from the experimental to ballads such as 'Yesterday'.

INVENTION AND TECHNOLOGY

A major step forward was made in 1960 when the laser was invented. An acronym for Light Amplification by Stimulated Emission of Radiation, the device produces a narrow beam of light that can travel for vast distances and is focused to give enormous power. Laser beams, as well as being able to carry far more information than radio waves, can also be used for surgery, cutting, drilling, welding and scores of other operations.

SCIENCE AND DISCOVERY

When the drug Thalidomide was first developed during the 1950s it was hailed as a wonder drug which would ease the distressing symptoms of pregnancy sickness. By the early 1960s the drug's terrible side effects were being discovered, when more than 3000 babies had been born with severe birth defects. Malformed limbs, defective eyes and faulty intestines were the heart-rending legacy left by Thalidomide.

By courtesy of Edinburgh City Libraries

It was a Saturday afternoon one day in the winter of 1930 when an intrepid cameraman took to the air over Edinburgh and from the west of the city swooped over Roseburn and Dalry. The main railway line into the heart of the city disappears into the top left hand side of the picture whilst the line cutting the picture diagonally in half has now disappeared entirely. And talking of hearts, there in the top centre of the scene is the Hearts of Midlothian football ground with the players out of the field, though it must be said with rather few supporters in the stands on this chilly day. How many readers however have spent happy afternoons cheering on the terraces with woolly hats and scarves to keep them warm in those carefree pre-war days. How many readers in later years stood on the terraces and cheered on their team with wooden rattles? And come to think of it whatever happened to wooden rattles at football grounds? To the left of the football ground is Tyncastle School where many thousands of Edinburgh children learned common sense, whilst below is the North British Distillery which, according to some, aimed in due course to deprive them of it! Cutting across the top right hand corner of the picture is Gorgie Road - the A71 whilst snaking brilliantly along the bottom of the picture and under the railway line is Roseburn Street on its way to Murrayfield away to the left.

Though no date is recorded for this aerial photograph of the Mayfield area of Edinburgh to the South East of Edinburgh it is believed to have been taken in the 1930s. At the bottom of the picture can be seen the circle of Waverley Park, above it Minto Street and Mayfair Gardens cuts across the scene whilst the upper left hand corner of the picture is bisected by Findhorn Place with Causewayside in the middle. This southern suburb of Edinburgh is seldom visited by tourists who spend their time around Old Town and the castle or prefer the shops and architectural delights of New Town, yet in many respects it is areas like this which are the real heart of modern Edinburgh. Here are the homes of real people, ordinary folk who for generations have made Edinburgh function; the folk who travel into the town to work in offices, shops, banks and government buildings yet return home each evening to the quiet anonymity which all of us crave in our private lives. Old Edinburgh had a population of perhaps 100,000. The industrial revolution would eventually see the population rise to four times that figure, creating increased demand for housing far beyond the boundaries envisaged by those who planned New Town. These homes to the south were built on a fine scale. What a pity that standard could not have been maintained in the 20th century and spared the Edinburgh skyline the blot of multi-storey tower blocks - though happily such architectural excrescences are fewer than in other British cities of comparable size.

Making a living

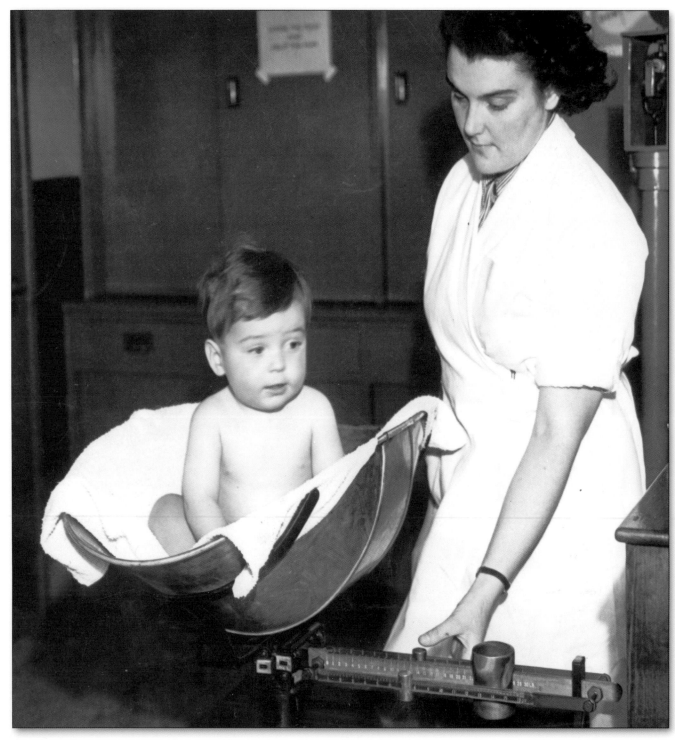

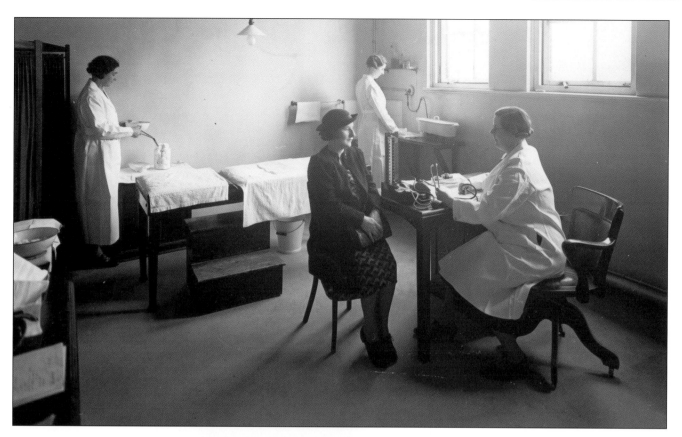

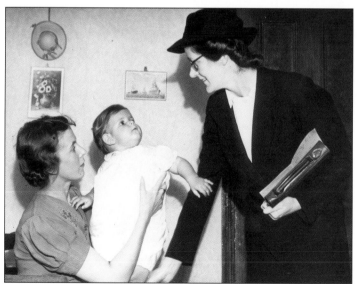

Both pages: It was possibly the acute wartime shortages of food and supplies which made doctors, health workers and mothers alike very aware of the health of the new generation, and children were carefully weighed, measured and immunised against the illnesses that had at one time meant disfigurement or even death *(facing page)*. A vaccine for polio, the scourge of former years which left behind its terrible mark of wasted and useless limbs, only came later, however. American scientist Jonas Edward Salk developed a vaccine in 1955, and an oral vaccine was produced in 1960. The vaccines brought the dreaded disease under control and today polio is rarely seen. On a day to day basis, vitamins were vital to the health of children, and long before the advent of the cod liver oil capsule, the recommended spoonful of cod liver oil was administered to the youngest children every day in schools and nurseries around the country during the 1940s. Children might have screwed up their noses at the fishy taste, but the nourishing cod liver oil went a long way towards keeping them healthy. The vitamin-packed orange juice was far more palatable, and artful mothers would often use the orange juice as a bribe: no cod liver oil, no orange juice. Following hard on the heels of the oil, the juice took away the distinctive taste that was disliked by so many children. Ante-natal clinics did all they could to check on the diet, blood pressure and vitamin intake of mothers to be; our carefully posed photograph, taken in an ante-natal clinic in the 1930s, records at least the cleanliness and tidiness that was to their great credit *(top)*. And when the tiny new citizen finally arrived, there were health visitors to pay friendly calls on families in their homes to check on the health and happiness of mothers and babies *(left)*. National Dried Milk for babies was also made available to mothers, and before today's push towards natural feeding NDM was for decades very much in vogue. We need to remember that at the time of these photographs the National Health service did not exist, and in fact the NHS only came into operation after World War II in July 1948.

Newhaven next to Leith docks is almost unknown outside Edinburgh yet in the 1930s within the city it was very well known for its mussel sellers who were often seen with their wicker baskets selling their seafood to passers by. This old dear has set up her stall in the gutter in Dundee Street with a short plank across the baskets on which she has plates, salt, vinegar and pepper laid out for the delectation of the three small boys who have gone to buy a penny's worth from her. Such street vendors had been a normal sight in Edinburgh since time immemorial - and no requirement then for a health and safety certificate. Looking back it's remarkable how little capital was need to set up a small business like this, and many folk did so; profits may not have been large but in the hungry thirties every penny counted, and selling fresh seafood on the streets of Edinburgh for a small profit often meant the difference between poverty and actual starvation. Seafood of course continues to be popular but the last mussel seller of this kind must have disappeared with the second world war to be replaced in the 1960s by hot dog salesman with custom made heated carts. Today the young lads pictured here must be well into their 70s, but even after all the passing years it's a fair bet that from time to time they suddenly get an urge for some seafood, though only to be disappointed by what they end up with - today's offerings simply won't taste the same as they did all those years ago, things never do.

Events of the 1930s

HOT OFF THE PRESS

The years of the 1930s saw Adolf Hitler's sickening anti-Jewish campaign echoed in the streets of Britain. On 19th October 1936 Oswald Mosley's 7,000-strong British Union of Fascists clashed head on with thousands of Jews and Communists in London, resulting in 80 people being injured in the ensuing battle. Mosley and his 'blackshirts' later rampaged through the streets beating up Jews and smashing the windows of their businesses.
A dark day in our country's history.

THE WORLD AT LARGE

In India, Gandhi's peaceful protests against British rule were gathering momentum. The Salt Laws were a great bone of contention: forced to buy salt from the British government, thousands of protestors marched to the salt works, intending to take it over in the name of the Indian people. Policemen and guards attacked the marchers, but not one of them fought back. Gandhi, who earned for himself the name 'Mahatma' - Great Soul - was assassinated in 1948.

ROYAL WATCH

The talking point of the early 1930s was the affair of the Prince of Wales, who later became King Edward VIII, and American divorcee Wallis Simpson. Faced with a choice, Edward gave up his throne for 'the woman I love' and spent the remainder of his life in exile. Many supported him, though they might not have been as keen to do so if they had been aware of his Nazi sympathies, kept strictly under wraps at the time.

Above: Johnston Terrace running along the south side of Edinburgh Castle is the scene of this photograph thought to have been taken in the 1930s. But what's going on? To young eyes the scene is a bit of a mystery; what are those mushroom-like objects the workmen are laying out in the road? The workmen are in fact engaged in 'studding'. In the days before white lines and yellow lines metal studs were frequently placed in roads to mark junctions or boundaries. Compared to the modern line painting equipment this was a slow, expensive and laborious undertaking. First the line had to be marked by a surveyor, following which a hole had to be chiselled in the road surface - the activity which is the central

By courtesy of Edinburgh City Libraries

By courtesy of Edinburgh City Libraries

Above: Proud Stationmaster Reg Dempster is pictured here in part of the garden at Morningside Road station on September 19th 1955 - the station garden regularly won prizes for its plants and flowers. Whatever happened to railway staff who actually dressed the part? Reg Demspster is not only wearing a proper peaked cap as part of his uniform it even has the words 'Station Master' along its brim. Uniforms like this were replaced in the 1960s with clothes which appeared to be designed for Chairman Mao's Red Guards, whilst these days with unmanned stations proliferating it's often hard to find any staff let alone a genuine Stationmaster like this. Back in the glory days of the railways when this picture was taken rail was still king. The first motorway had yet to be built and the notion of taking an aeroplane was an incredible luxury, and something only rich folk did. The first overseas package holiday to Spain had yet to take off and a trip to the seaside by train was the most that the majority of Edinburgh folk aspired to. The journeys may have been short but what a high standard of service was on offer. If you needed it railway staff would even call at your home to collect your trunk and deliver it to your destination before you arrived. These days there's little chance of even finding a porter to carry a single suitcase to a taxi.

feature of this picture as one man kneels holding the cold chisel whilst a second hefts a sledgehammer. Nearest to us are the studs waiting to be used, trailing into the distance are a line of studs already hammered into the ground by a third workman half hidden behind his colleagues. The man with his hands in his pockets is undoubtedly the foreman - that always imperious figure for whom the classic lines were composed about no longer being a member of the working class! Though metal studs remained an oft seen feature of the street scene until the 1960s they were not only relatively costly but also dangerous: the metal could be very slippy and they would be blamed for many car accidents in which the driver would claim that he lost control after skidding on them.

Above: In 1957 the people of Edinburgh gathered in large numbers to give a rousing farewell to the men of the 603 (City of Edinburgh) Squadron Royal Auxiliary Air Force as they parade their squadron standard across Waverley Bridge for the very last time. As they march over the bridge the men give a smart 'eyes left' to the Lord Provost of Edinburgh. Many years before the outbreak of the second world war in 1939 Lord Trenchard had envisaged a Reserve Air Force in which yeomanry units were recruited and trained near to their homes. The Squadron's headquarters were at 25 Learmouth Terrace in the heart of the city. Both the bomber and fighter squadrons of 603 had their headquarters at number 25 along with support unit 2603 (Light AA Regiment Unit) and 3603 (Fighter Control Unit). Edinburgh's link with the Royal Auxiliary Air Force would long remain in Learmouth Terrace, which in 1959 became the Maritime Headquarters Unit made up of members of the disbanded 603 Squadron and the 3603 Fighter Control Unit. Thought the war may have ended in 1945 it took many years for it consequences to wind down. This photograph marks the disbanding of the 603 Squadron a dozen years after the end of World War II. In March 1957, to commemorate those who served in it, a memorial plaque dedicated to 603 Squadron was erected opposite the gates of the now-closed RAF Turnhouse. Another memorial would be a full-scale fibreglass replica of a Spitfire at Edinburgh Airport.

Managing the millions

Ivory & Sime had a presence in Edinburgh's traditional Georgian Charlotte Square since the firm was founded in 1895 as an accountancy practice by James Ivory and Thomas Sime. Friends Provident is even older having been founded by Quakers in 1832.

Today ISIS is one of the ten largest asset management companies in the UK. Its shares are quoted on the London stock exchange, and with approximately £60 billion under its management it is strongly positioned as one of the few fund managers with sufficient critical mass to prosper in a rapidly changing marketplace.

The company is a major player in retail and industrial markets and has strong presence in equity, fixed interest, private equity and property markets. ISIS also manages insurance funds for Friends Provident and Royal & Sun Alliance.

ISIS employs around 500 staff of which over 120 are investment professionals. In addition to its prestigious premises in Edinburgh the company has offices in London, Manchester, Birmingham and Dorking.

The Scotsman who is careful with his money is a national stereotype recognised throughout the world. In fact many Scots have also been renowned for their generosity and benevolence; but it's being noted for watching the pennies that makes Edinburgh very attractive as a base for financial institutions anxious to share Scotland's unrivalled reputation for fiscal good sense.

In 2003 ISIS Asset Management Plc, one of the UK's foremost financial institutions, moved to new premises at 80 George Street from where it invests large sums of money on behalf of its clients.

It was only in September 2002 that ISIS had been formed as a result of the integration of Friends, Ivory & Sime with Royal & Sun Alliance Investments. Friends, Ivory & Sime was itself the result of a merger between the fund management arm of Friends Provident and Edinburgh-based Ivory & Sime in 1998.

On the face of it ISIS is a new company, but it can trace its roots to a long and distinguished past.

Top: The company premises, 80 George Street. **Above right**: *Charlotte Square, home of Ivory and Sime from 1895-2003.* **Right**: *A view of Edinburgh Castle from 80 George Street.*

Learning to live

Today the most significant name in further education in Edinburgh is that of Telford College. The origins of the further education system in Edinburgh can be traced back to a very precise date: 13th September 1894. On that day a separate evening school was opened at the Regent Road Public School for girls over the age of 14. Classes were offered in academic subjects such as English, arithmetic, bookkeeping and commercial geography - in addition to dressmaking, needlework and singing. Such continuation classes were intended purely as a winter activity and ended each March. By 1898, the number of students attending had reached 223 with classes in science, French, shorthand and domestic economy added to original courses.

The 13th winter session held in 1906 began under new conditions - young men and lads were now also offered the opportunity to attend: by 1910 the number of enrolments rose to 452.

By tradition Scotland had leaned towards literacy and academic education during the day and technical education in the evening. By the 1940s however the importance of day release classes was being recognised. The first day continuation classes for hairdressers began as early as 1944 at

Regent Road, whilst later that same year a class for young civil servants began at the Torphichen Street Day Institute. Over the next three years further day release classes would be offered: pre-apprentice courses for prospective engineering apprentices, commercial classes for disabled men, classes for 'mentally defective girls', classes for apprentice grocers as well as for Post Office Telegraph Messengers or 'junior postmen' as they were later called.

A School of Housepainting and Decorating was opened in the former St James School, Broughton Street when the College of Art could no longer cope with the numbers.

By 1950, day release classes at Regent Road had expanded to accommodate all junior civil servants between the ages of 15 and 18, teaching them not only English and maths but also history, geography, citizenship, handwriting and French. That same year apprentice builders were introduced at New Street, where 52 joiners, 64 housepainters, 46 plumbers and 22 glaziers were accommodated. By 1951, 125 young employees of St Cuthbert's Co-operative Association were enjoying the privilege of day release in five classes of 25. Many more

Top: *Regent Road - beginning of the road to Telford.*
Right: *The Coat of Arms of the former Edinburgh Corporation can still be seen above the main entrance of the College's North Campus. Roughly translated the wording means 'Without the Lord in vain'.* **Far right:** *WM Ramsay Technical Institute, the base for the Department of Engineering*

increasing emphasis on piecework meant fewer tradesmen had the time to train youngsters.

The new Act set up some 17 Industrial Training Boards, of which those of the Construction Industry (CITB) and the Engineering Industry (EITB) would have the most influence at Telford College. The new courses were funded by financial levies imposed by the Boards on their respective industries - and in turn those industries could employ those apprentices with no additional educational cost.

Robert McLeod took up his duties as Principal in August 1966, before the College existed in a physical sense: the map of the College in 1967-68 indeed featured lots of annexes but no actual main building.

businesses would in due course also be persuaded to send their young employees along.

After 1945 there was a call for local technical colleges specially designed and built for the purpose of further education.

Of the district 'craft level' colleges Telford would be Edinburgh's first. The College opened at Crewe Toll on 26th August 1968 - exactly one year late because of a government freeze on spending. The original cost was to be £1,287,000 but Edinburgh Corporation subsequently agreed to add £273,000 for an extension capable of taking an additional 1,500 day release building students.

The driving force behind the further education building programme of the 1960s was the 1964 Industrial Training Act which arose from a belief that the traditional apprenticeship of serving one's time making tea and running errands was no longer working, not least because an

When complete, the new College would take on Junior Commerce work from the Torphichen Street Institute as well as the Retail Distribution Trades Section from New Street. For the time being however, the Department of Engineering would continue to be based at the WM Ramsay Technical Institute at Inchview Terrace, Portobello.

The WM Ramsay Technical Institute had a curious history. Built in 1906 as a chocolate factory by a German immigrant, the building was rumoured to be a hotbed of German spies when war broke out in 1914. Though there was no evidence of spying the unfortunate German manager was interned for the duration of the war and the building requisitioned by the military until 1919.

Subsequently the building was handed over to the Ministry of Labour which turned it into a Government Industrial Factory where disabled ex-servicemen

Top left: Young Coopers mastering their trade at Ramsay Tech in 1963. **Above:** *Tutor, Brian Rockett is extremely watchful as a young apprentice operates the planing machine.* **Above right:** *Torphichen Street Institute, which became an annexe of Edinburgh College of Commerce in 1966.* **Right:** *Principal McLeod receives the Hambledon Trophy presented by The British Display Society, the first of many awards won by Telford Art & Design students.*

Pre-apprenticeship courses in engineering were introduced at Ramsay Tech in 1945. Two years later, day release courses were being offered for apprentices in the motor vehicle trade, followed by similar courses for trainee miners and engineers.

After courses and staff were transferred to the new complex at Crewe Toll in 1968 the Ramsay Tech building was used as a Youth Hostel for two years before becoming an annexe to Stevenson College until it was sold in 1995 to be converted into residential flats.

The new College would offer a remarkable range of courses, and as demand increased so did the pressure on space. In 1988 the Lothian Regional Council Education Committee recommended the development of a two-site campus in order to take advantage of underused accommodation at Ainslie Park High School - a development which would also facilitate the closure of annexes at Ferry Road, Granton and Lochend.

could be trained as craftsmen. As part of the practical work some of the disabled students built a cottage, No 72 Inchview Terrace.

The industrial factory was bought by the School Board in 1923 for £13,000 to use for apprentice training, and renamed the WM Ramsay Technical School. Woodworking, pattern making, vehicle building and tailoring were soon being offered with some 716 students enrolled at the 'Ramsay Tech' by 1923-24. Along with the Tynecastle Workshops the 'Tech' became the main provider of non-advanced craft training in engineering and specialist aspects of woodworking. The building's prominent position was recognised during the second world war when a light anti-aircraft battery was mounted on the roof.

The proposal was not entirely magnanimous; it would help the Education Committee out of a thorny problem since school rolls had fallen dramatically at Ainslie Park. In June 1991 the school was merged with Broughton High and the Ainslie Park complex was taken over by Telford College - though not without some protest from parents who mistakenly believed that the whole exercise had been a ploy by the College to close 'their' school.

The Ainslie Park site would in future become the Telford College North campus.

Pressure on accommodation however continued, especially for advanced course work and commercial

Top left: Students sit their exams in the College's Sports Hall. Above right: The South frontage of the College's North Campus with the pre-fabricated buildings which became the home of the College Nursery in 1999 to the right. Below: The former playing field at South Campus. Right: The Darwin Maze, intended to demonstrate Charles Darwin's Theory of Evolution, was created at Edinburgh Zoo, with bricklayers, joiners, plasterers, masons and plumbers all taking part in the construction of a visitors' picnic shelter, toilet facilities and a terraced area.

seven 'teaching schools: building & engineering; business; care, health & the sciences; communication; computing & office technology; creative arts and leisure industries.

Over the years there has been a decline in demand for building and engineering courses - and the virtual disappearance of general education which had been an integral part of all City & Guild craft courses; there had however been a compensatory rise in demand for creative arts and leisure industry courses. In the 1980s the College largely provided courses at National Certificate level with few Higher National Certificates (HNC) and Diplomas (HND): by the mid 1990s some 30 per cent of the College's work was at this level as demand for higher qualifications had increased.

Meanwhile the 1992 Further and Higher Education (Scotland) Act would lead to the most significant event in the College's history. The enormous potential of the College and the enthusiasm of its staff were released by turning the College into a free standing corporate body, independent of the Lothian Regional Council and making it for the first time an autonomous body capable of making its own decisions about its future.

activities. Eventually attention focused on a modern three storey office block in Telford Road which had previously been used by various companies including Ferranti. The building would become the College's West campus in 1994.

By 1998, after 30 years of existence, Telford College was truly bursting at the seams. The original 7,300 students had grown to 17,315 of which some 2,724 were now full-time students. Courses were offered by

Today, under its Principal Dr Ray Harris, the College currently has 21,500 students and 750 staff. The future includes a brand new campus, with construction starting in 2003-4, to create the best possible environment for both working and learning.

Top and above left:*The new Dance Studio (top left) which was converted from the traditional School Gymnasium (above left) in 1995.* ***Left:*** *A birds eye view of Telford College in 1968.* ***Below:*** *The entrance of Edinburgh's Telford College, 2003.*

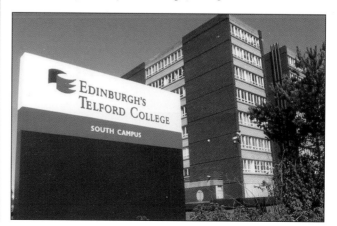

The ultimate service

According to the old adage there are only two certainties in life - death and taxes. The very rich and the very poor may avoid taxes, but none of us avoid death. And if the manner of our passing may matter little to us once we are gone it is very important to the bereaved.

They want not only to see us end our days with dignity but also to see that their final farewells are made with fitting decorum. Until the 19th century however few funerals for ordinary folk left their mark. Our great churches and cathedrals were, and still are, filled with the effigies of, and memorials to, the great and the good, but most ordinary people had to be content with much less. For the average man or woman laying out would be conducted by a local woman who was probably a neighbour who did this important job on a part time basis - and often doubled up as a midwife. The local carpenter would make a coffin and the burial in the local churchyard would, like as not, be marked with a simple wooden cross which would disappear in a few years time.

The demand for elaborate funerals reached its height in the Victorian era, as witnessed by the many elaborate memorials in Edinburgh's graveyards. And with that funerary elaboration rose the profession of modern undertaker.

Few firms of funeral directors were founded quite as long ago as the Victorian Age, but Thomas Marin Funeral Directors, based in Edinburgh's St Mary's Street, nevertheless has an impressive pedigree which goes back to the 1920s.

Since its establishment in 1926 Thomas Marin Funeral Directors has passed from one generation of the Marin family to the next, making the firm not just a business but a true family concern.

Above: *Founder, Thomas 'Tommy' Marin.*
Right: *The company premises at 64 St Mary's Street pictured in the 1960s.*

The original Thomas Marin, known as Tommy, bought his funeral directors business from a Mr Crian back in the 1920s.

A graduate of the College of Art in Edinburgh Tommy was actually a professional engraver with no experience of being an undertaker, but his commitment and determination, coupled with the help of the clergy in Edinburgh and the local population, meant that he soon found out what people wanted at funerals.

For a number of years Tommy, his wife Cissie, and their family, lived at the back of the shop in St Mary's

Street: they would work tirelessly to build up the business and to make sure that the service they gave to every customer was of the highest quality.

Tommy continually strove to improve his services: he joined the National Association of Funeral Directors as well as the British Institute of Embalmers, becoming one of the first funeral directors in Scotland to pass the latter's examinations and practice the art of preservation.

When the second world war arrived Tommy found his skills being called upon by the American Forces who appointed him to take care of their casualties in Scotland, an indication of Tommy's rising reputation in the business.

Now semi-retired, Tommy's son Jim recalls that his father had a good head for business as well as a strong desire to put the customer first. Tommy was a man who in the very early days saw that the telephone was a vital instrument in the undertaking business, often saying that the firm was always as near as the nearest telephone and even using it to establish contact with the local population by putting a notice in the window inviting people to use the office phone.

To this day the telephone at Thomas Marin's is manned every hour of the day and night 365 days a year by the firm's staff - answering machines simply do not suit a company which prides itself on its personal touch.

Jim Marin joined his father in 1948 after doing his National Service. Jim would never forget his years of hard work as an apprentice under Tommy's strict regime, a philosophy which required everything about the company to be precise and professional.

That stern training would stand Jim, and later his son Iain and daughter Jane, in good stead to enable them to continue to serve the communities in the Lothian area to the same high standards as its founder had demanded.

After a career in teaching, which took him to London and Casablanca as well as Edinburgh, Iain Marin joined his father in the expanding family firm in the 1980s. In 1984 the firm

Top: *James Scott's furniture shop in the 1950s.*
Above: *Tommy Marin (left) pictured with his family; daughter in law Pat, son Jim, daughter Joan and wife Cissie.*

acquired the funeral side of the business of James Scott & Son, Furniture Suppliers, Portobello though retaining the name and employing the Scott resident funereal director Ian Dunbar.

Jim Marin's daughter Jane, formerly a qualified nursery nurse, is a relatively recent addition to the firm.

Merging these two businesses combined with the arrival of Iain Marin would prove advantageous to all, not least with the rationalisation of facilities, for example by handling all the clerical work and record keeping at St Mary's Street.

Meanwhile the firm has always been conscious of the need to invest in the best modern, up-to-date sanitary equipment as well as more recently hi-tech computer software which is essential to the day to day running of the business.

Since the days when Tommy Marin first entered the business the company has continuously been involved in preserving the bodies of the deceased, something which is desirable both from the point of view of hygiene as well as an important presentation factor for families who would understandably like to view the remains in near perfect conditions.

In pursuit of its aim of perfection the firm employs no less than three certified technicians and has built a modern and superbly equipped preparation room.

More than 20 years ago Jim introduced computers to the business but is still battling with its complexities. The one principal he has learned however when dealing with computers is that they should work for you and not the other way around. But being admittedly a little old fashioned Jim still insists on keeping written records, and is proud to be able to add them to the files which go back to 1926.

Those records from the early days of the business have proved invaluable to families of the Scottish diaspora who have moved to Canada, Australasia and elsewhere and who often get in touch with the firm which is more than happy to furnish them with details of relatives who died long ago.

Meanwhile the business principles first established by Tommy Marin have continued down the decades,

Top left: *Cardinal Gray's coffin is lowered into the vault in St Mary's Cathedral.* ***Top right:*** *The funeral of Lord John Wheatley at St Peter's Catholic Church, Morningside, July 1988.* ***Left:*** *James Scott Portobello acquired by the company in 1984.*

enabling this family-owned firm with its caring and reliable service to draw on a wealth of tradition and experience enabling it to provide funerals that are personal, respectful and value for money. Marin funerals have ranged from that of a travelling woman whose coffin was transported in a glass carriage to the solemn and pious funeral of the late Cardinal Gordon Gray who died in July 1993.

'Burying people you know is the hardest part of the job' Jim Marin would recall after the funeral of Cardinal Gray who was a friend of his. 'But although we always strive to be professional here we don't like to be too solemn, so I insist on the men wearing grey suits instead of black'

'People often comment on the friendly, family atmosphere we have here and that is what we aim to maintain'.

'We are dealing with people when they are at their most vulnerable but is also when they are at their strongest.

We see the best of people here and that is why it is such a privilege to be working in the business'.

'Every funeral we organise is special whether it is in a church, a chapel, a crematorium or at one of our private facilities in a funeral parlour, we can take care of everything'.

During the course of nine decades the firm of Thomas Marin Funeral Directors has been providing the people of Edinburgh with the kind of funeral they would wish for themselves and for their loved ones. Edinburgh folk are not mawkish or over sentimental but they do have a long tradition of giving death the quiet respect it deserves and marking that final transition with due dignity. Generations have trusted Thomas Marin and his family with making those final arrangements - and none have been disappointed with the professional and understanding manner with which the firm has provided this, the ultimate service.

Top: One of the St Mary's Street viewing rooms.
Left: Long-serving members of staff, June, Bill (left) and Steve. Below: Bill and Steve with a hearse and limousine from the company's extensive fleet of vehicles.

Link - working together, providing homes, building communities

Link Housing Association Ltd was formed in 1962 by a group of business and professional people with experience and interest in housing. Link's aim was 'to carry on the industry, business and trade of providing housing for letting and any associated amenities in Scotland'.

The name Link was chosen because the houses to be built would help fill the gap between owner-occupation and council housing.

Within four years Link had already constructed over 200 new dwellings for families to rent in Edinburgh and Polmont. Three of those developments received Saltire Awards for design.

At the same time, Link was active in the provision of small flats for older people. All of those properties were located in the City, the majority being in the New Town. Loans were obtained from Edinburgh Corporation to subdivide large town houses.

Right: *Queensferry Road, Edinburgh.*
Below: *Barnton, Edinburgh.*

Link would go on to develop in many parts of the country, notably in the Central Belt but also as far as Kyle of Lochalsh and Coldstream.

Link has also helped other housing associations. Port of Leith Housing Association was set up in 1975 and was serviced initially by Link's staff and members. After one year Port of Leith was able to become independent with full-time staff of its own and become a major contributor to the revitalisation of Edinburgh's port.

Changing family patterns have meant that Link needed to place greater emphasis on housing to meet the needs of single people, older people and people with disabilities.

In partnership with health and social work departments and local community-based voluntary organisations, Link has also

officers and welfare rights staff to work with tenants to improve their quality of life.

The millennium saw the completion of 95 new homes at Comely Green Place in Edinburgh for rent, sale, shared ownership and community care needs. This project was designed to minimise the adverse effects of new developments on the environment and to reduce the running costs for residents. The project was recognised by the Chartered Institute of Housing in Scotland, which gave it a '2000 Scottish Housing and Innovation Award' for environmental building and best practice.

Today the Link group of companies comprises: the Link Group - the 'Parent', Link Housing - managing Link's social rented stock, Linkwide - developing sustainable communities, LinkLiving - supporting people in their homes, Link Property - providing property and estate management and factoring, and Link Homes, building homes for sale.

catered for young people, those with mental health problems and people with learning disabilities. Projects for people with hearing or visual impairments were also established.

1981 saw the introduction of 'Shared Ownership'. Link assumed a pioneering role being one of only four associations involved in the first programme, buying 48 properties throughout Central Scotland. Since then Link has acquired or developed nearly 600 dwellings for this type of tenure.

Link Housing Association itself was precluded from providing housing for sale and for market rent: in 1985 a subsidiary, Link Homes Ltd, was formed to perform those functions. Link Homes has provided over 500 low-cost, high quality homes for sale and market rent.

Partnership working has been fundamental. One example was the project at St John's Hill, Edinburgh completed in 1998. Through a partnership between Link, Edinvar and Haven Housing Associations and the Edinburgh Council for Single Homeless, it provided 67 new homes and a Day Centre.

Another Partnership initiative has been in Niddrie/Craigmillar. A consortium involving four housing associations acting in partnership with the local community and the City of Edinburgh Council helping regenerate the area by providing 500 new or improved homes. Participants in the project have adopted the title 'Kintry' ('neighbourhood' in Old Scots).

Link is committed to involving its customers in running its business and employs tenant liaison

Since its formation Link has been in the forefront of the introduction of new housing initiatives in Scotland. The group aims to develop over 100 new or refurbished homes each year, and with some 6,500 properties and over 300 staff, the Link Group looks set fair to continue to develop many new areas of housing services and community regeneration.

Top left: Dean Village, Edinburgh.
Above left: Royal Circus, Edinburgh.
Left: Cramond, Edinburgh.

A class outfit

So where did you get taken for your school clothes? If you were taken to be kitted out for school in the 1940s the answer to that that question might be any one of a dozen well known Edinburgh stores; but if you were lucky you may have been taken to the best of them all: Aitken & Niven.

Founded in 1905 at 46 Queensferry Street by Robert Aitken and his wife (whose maiden name had been Niven) as a tailors and outfitters for Edinburgh gentlemen the firm of Aitken & Niven quickly acquired a strong reputation amongst Edinburgh society for quality and service. It was an unwavering commitment to those core values which enabled the firm to survive the difficult and erratic economic climate of its first few decades.

Above: *William Ferguson.*
Below: *Aitken & Niven's Queensferry Street premises in the 1950s.* **Right:** *William Ferguson's letter of resignation as Senior Salesman of the Gentlemen's and Boys' Outfitting Department of Jenners, 1943.*

In 1943 William Ferguson, the grandfather of the company's current Managing Director, joined the business after approaching the founder with the idea of setting up a School Outfitters Department within the store. The new department proved to be very popular, and as a result William Ferguson now became a partner. Robert Aitken retired in 1949 and the store passed into the ownership of the Ferguson family, though retaining its original name. As a private limited company it had around 20 shareholders who owned a third of the shares whilst the remaining two thirds were held by the Ferguson family.

William Ferguson's son Derek joined his father in 1956. With business rapidly increasing after the austerity of the immediate post war years the company was now able to move from Queensferry Street to a more central location, occupying 79 George Street in 1958.

Sadly, in 1964, William Ferguson passed away and his son Derek succeeded him as Managing Director. Under

Derek Ferguson's effective guidance the firm prospered and developed throughout the 1960s, 70s and 80s.

These were decades when most shops were becoming 'self-service', and independent department stores were becoming an increasingly rare sight in city centres: but Derek Ferguson continued to put his faith in Aitken & Niven's long-standing values of quality and service, and as a direct result of continuing to follow that credo the store continued to grow.

As the business became increasingly successful new departments were opened including sportswear and sports equipment, a natural extension of the school-wear market. In 1980 the store expanded next door into 77 George Street, a development which allowed more new departments, featuring ladies fashions, babies wear and footwear to open. These were soon followed by an in-store restaurant.

In the mid 1980s David Ferguson, Derek Ferguson's son and the grandson of William Ferguson, joined the company. The early 1990s saw a decision to expand and take the name of Aitken & Niven further afield. In 1991 the company bought Fenwicks Department Store in Perth, and in 1993 it acquired the Alan Mickel shoe shop in Glasgow.

David Ferguson became Managing Director in 1996 when his father Derek retired. Since then there have been many changes, not least the development of new departments such as Trutex and Canterbury as well as the introduction of closed circuit TV in the store.

A new branch of Aitken & Niven was opened in Falcon Road in Morning to the South West of Edinburgh in 2001, whilst in 2002 the firm opened its 'Canterbury of New Zealand' store in Edinburgh's Rose Street.

Aitken & Niven is now one of the few remaining independently owned department stores in Scotland, and one of only two schools outfitters in Edinburgh. The store now consists of seven departments spread over three floors.

The company has established a corporate image for all its stores utilising the distinctive Aitken & Niven colours of black and gold, and today it receives s sales enquiries from across the globe. Those sales however are no longer primarily focused on school outfits. In the early 1980s school outfits still comprised 85 per cent of Aitken and Niven's sales, but by the early years of the 21st century that proportion had fallen to just 35 per cent - perhaps not surprising when the firm's sportswear department alone now proudly boasts the largest independent collection of rugby wear and equipment in the world.

Left: 79 George Street circa 1958.
Above: Advertising of school uniforms and the company's rugby mail order catalogue.

Acknowledgments

The publishers would like to thank the following, who have kindly allowed us to use photographs from the collection held at Edinburgh Central Library:

Stuart Sellar
Francis Caird Inglis
Stanley George Jackman
Langley Pearce Bain
Edinburgh Photographic Society
J. Campbell Harper
A. Harper
James A. Tait

Also thanks to the staff of The Edinburgh Room at Edinburgh Central Library

As always thanks are due to Andrew Mitchell and Steve Ainsworth

True North Books Ltd - Book List

Memories of Accrington - 1 903204 05 4

Memories of Barnet - 1 903204 16 X

Memories of Barnsley - 1 900463 11 3

Golden Years of Barnsley -1 900463 87 3

Memories of Basingstoke - 1 903204 26 7

Memories of Bedford - 1 900463 83 0

More Memories of Bedford - 1 903204 33 X

Golden Years of Birmingham - 1 900463 04 0

Birmingham Memories - 1 903204 45 3

Memories of Blackburn - 1 900463 40 7

More Memories of Blackburn - 1 900463 96 2

Memories of Blackpool - 1 900463 21 0

Memories of Bolton - 1 900463 45 8

More Memories of Bolton - 1 900463 13 X

Bolton Memories - 1 903204 37 2

Memories of Bournemouth -1 900463 44 X

Memories of Bradford - 1 900463 00 8

More Memories of Bradford - 1 900463 16 4

More Memories of Bradford II - 1 900463 63 6

Bradford Memories - 1 903204 47 X

Bradford City Memories - 1 900463 57 1

Memories of Bristol - 1 900463 78 4

More Memories of Bristol - 1 903204 43 7

Memories of Bromley - 1 903204 21 6

Memories of Burnley - 1 900463 95 4

Golden Years of Burnley - 1 900463 67 9

Memories of Bury - 1 900463 90 3

Memories of Cambridge - 1 900463 88 1

Memories of Cardiff - 1 900463 14 8

More Memories of Cardiff - 1 903204 73 9

Memories of Carlisle - 1 900463 38 5

Memories of Chelmsford - 1 903204 29 1

Memories of Cheltenham - 1 903204 17 8

Memories of Chester - 1 900463 46 6

More Memories of Chester -1 903204 02 X

Memories of Chesterfield -1 900463 61 X

More Memories of Chesterfield - 1 903204 28 3

Memories of Colchester - 1 900463 74 1

Nostalgic Coventry - 1 900463 58 X

Coventry Memories - 1 903204 38 0

Memories of Croydon - 1 900463 19 9

More Memories of Croydon - 1 903204 35 6

Golden Years of Darlington - 1 900463 72 5

Nostalgic Darlington - 1 900463 31 8

Darlington Memories - 1 903204 46 1

Memories of Derby - 1 900463 37 7

More Memories of Derby - 1 903204 20 8

Memories of Dewsbury & Batley - 1 900463 80 6

Memories of Doncaster - 1 900463 36 9

Nostalgic Dudley - 1 900463 03 2

Golden Years of Dudley - 1 903204 60 7

Memories of Edinburgh - 1 900463 33 4

More memories of Edinburgh - 1903204 72 0

Memories of Enfield - 1 903204 14 3

Memories of Exeter - 1 900463 94 6

Memories of Glasgow - 1 900463 68 7

More Memories of Glasgow - 1 903204 44 5

Memories of Gloucester - 1 903204 04 6

Memories of Grimsby - 1 900463 97 0

More Memories of Grimsby - 1 903204 36 4

Memories of Guildford - 1 903204 22 4

Memories of Halifax - 1 900463 05 9

More Memories of Halifax - 1 900463 06 7

Golden Years of Halifax - 1 900463 62 8

Nostalgic Halifax - 1 903204 30 5

Memories of Harrogate - 1 903204 01 1

Memories of Hartlepool - 1 900463 42 3

Memories of High Wycombe - 1 900463 84 9

Memories of Huddersfield - 1 900463 15 6

More Memories of Huddersfield - 1 900463 26 1

Golden Years of Huddersfield - 1 900463 77 6

Nostalgic Huddersfield - 1 903204 19 4

Huddersfield Town FC - 1 900463 51 2

Memories of Hull - 1 900463 86 5

More Memories of Hull - 1 903204 06 2

Hull Memories - 1 903204 70 4

Memories of Ipswich - 1 900463 09 1

More Memories of Ipswich - 1 903204 52 6

Memories of Keighley - 1 900463 01 6

Golden Years of Keighley - 1 900463 92 X

Memories of Kingston - 1 903204 24 0

Memories of Leeds - 1 900463 75 X

True North Books Ltd - Book List

Memories of Kingston - 1 903204 24 0

Memories of Leeds - 1 900463 75 X

More Memories of Leeds - 1 900463 12 1

Golden Years of Leeds - 1 903204 07 0

Memories of Leicester - 1 900463 08 3

More Memories of Leicester - 1 903204 08 9

Memories of Leigh - 1 903204 27 5

Memories of Lincoln - 1 900463 43 1

Memories of Liverpool - 1 900463 07 5

More Memories of Liverpool - 1 903204 09 7

Liverpool Memories - 1 903204 53 4

Memories of Luton - 1 900463 93 8

Memories of Macclesfield - 1 900463 28 8

Memories of Manchester - 1 900463 27 X

More Memories of Manchester - 1 903204 03 8

Manchester Memories - 1 903204 54 2

Memories of Middlesbrough - 1 900463 56 3

More Memories of Middlesbrough - 1 903204 42 9

Memories of Newbury - 1 900463 79 2

Memories of Newcastle - 1 900463 81 4

More Memories of Newcastle - 1 903204 10 0

Newcastle Memories - 1.903204 71 2

Memories of Newport - 1 900463 59 8

Memories of Northampton - 1 900463 48 2

More Memories of Northampton - 1 903204 34 8

Memories of Norwich - 1 900463 73 3

Memories of Nottingham - 1 900463 91 1

More Memories of Nottingham - 1 903204 11 9

Bygone Oldham - 1 900463 25 3

Memories of Oldham - 1 900463 76 8

Memories of Oxford - 1 900463 54 7

Memories of Peterborough - 1 900463 98 9

Golden Years of Poole - 1 900463 69 5

Memories of Portsmouth - 1 900463 39 3

More Memories of Portsmouth - 1 903204 51 8

Nostalgic Preston - 1 900463 50 4

More Memories of Preston - 1 900463 17 2

Preston Memories - 1 903204 41 0

Memories of Reading - 1 900463 49 0

Memories of Rochdale - 1 900463 60 1

More Memories of Reading - 1 903204 39 9

More Memories of Rochdale - 1 900463 22 9

Memories of Romford - 1 903204 40 2

Memories of St Albans - 1 903204 23 2

Memories of St Helens - 1 900463 52 0

Memories of Sheffield - 1 900463 20 2

More Memories of Sheffield - 1 900463 32 6

Golden Years of Sheffield - 1 903204 13 5

Memories of Slough - 1 900 463 29 6

Golden Years of Solihull - 1 903204 55 0

Memories of Southampton - 1 900463 34 2

More Memories of Southampton - 1 903204 49 6

Memories of Stockport - 1 900463 55 5

More Memories of Stockport - 1 903204 18 6

Memories of Stockton - 1 900463 41 5

Memories of Stoke-on-Trent - 1 900463 47 4

More Memories of Stoke-on-Trent - 1 903204 12 7

Memories of Stourbridge - 1903204 31 3

Memories of Sunderland - 1 900463 71 7

More Memories of Sunderland - 1 903204 48 8

Memories of Swindon - 1 903204 00 3

Memories of Uxbridge - 1 900463 64 4

Memories of Wakefield - 1 900463 65 2

More Memories of Wakefield - 1 900463 89 X

Nostalgic Walsall - 1 900463 18 0

Golden Years of Walsall - 1 903204 56 9

More Memories of Warrington - 1 900463 02 4

Memories of Watford - 1 900463 24 5

Golden Years of West Bromwich - 1 900463 99 7

Memories of Wigan - 1 900463 85 7

Golden Years of Wigan - 1 900463 82 2

Nostalgic Wirral - 1 903204 15 1

Wirral Memories - 1 903204 747

Memories of Woking - 1 903204 32 1

Nostalgic Wolverhampton - 1 900463 53 9

Wolverhampton Memories - 1 903204 50 X

Memories of Worcester - 1 903204 25 9

Memories of Wrexham - 1 900463 23 7

Memories of York - 1 900463 66 0